D

"Ella Prichard has given us a gift in her deeply personal account of widowhood. In her new book, *Reclaiming Joy*, she lays the framework, through the book of Philippians, to experience God's presence and provision in times of grief and loss. It is at once practical, honest, hopeful, and encouraging. *Reclaiming Joy* is a beautiful chronicle of the strength, wisdom, and maturity that comes from enduring times of loss."

—ELIZABETH HEAD BLACK, author of *Hand in Hand: Walking with the Psalms through Loneliness*

"After forty-six years of marriage, Ella suddenly found herself widowed and thrust into a life she did not choose. *Reclaiming Joy* is an account of one brave woman's ability to navigate the most difficult journey of her life and help others who are trying to do the same. It is a one-step-at-a-time guide, resource, and affirmation of the hope that you can, one day, find your own joy."

—JACKIE BAUGH MOORE, Vice President, Eula Mae and John Baugh Foundation

"Open. Honest. Compelling. Ella Wall Prichard's journey through grief to acceptance to finding joy will give widows everywhere the confidence to believe that life can be good again. By telling her story, she offers hope to those in despair, encouragement to those feeling overwhelmed, and wisdom for those unsure of the next steps. A rich, practical, insightful read that invites every widow to choose life."

—REV. DR. GARY W. KLINGSPORN, Senior Minister, First Congregational Church, Nantucket, Massachusetts

"Ella Prichard is a courageous and insightful steward of grief who has produced a profound and uplifting book on joy. Her subtitle calls this book 'a primer for widows,' but it imparts wisdom for all who grieve the passing of someone they loved deeply."

—MARV KNOX, Field Coordinator, Fellowship Southwest, Coppell, Texas

"'Joy comes with the morning,' the psalmist says, after the night of mourning. In *Reclaiming Joy*, Ella Wall Prichard teaches us something else that is only learned in the crucible of grief and loss. Joy that comes with the morning is only possible by seeking joy in the mourning."

—GEORGE MASON, Senior Pastor, Wilshire
Baptist Church, Dallas, Texas

"In *Reclaiming Joy*, Ella Wall Prichard invites you into her honest, courageous, and vulnerable journey of rediscovering a life filled with meaning and purpose after the death of her husband. Her profound insights will inspire and encourage you to find joy again regardless of the pain and losses on your own journey."

—JIMMY DORRELL, Co-founder and
President, Mission Waco

RECLAIMING
JOY

a primer for widows

Ella Wall Prichard

1845BOOKS

Cover Design by Savanah N. Landerholm

Cover photograph cropped from "Surf Check" (©2016)
by Michael Gaillard, www.michaelgaillard.com,
studio@michaelgaillard.com

Parts of chapters 1, 7, and 17 of the present work appeared in a
somewhat different version in "From Grief to Joy: Rebuilding
an Abundant Life," *Women and Wealth Magazine,* Summer
2016, 18–21. © 2016 by Brown Brothers Harriman. Used with
permission.

Unless otherwise noted, all Scripture is from the New Revised
Standard Version of the Bible.

This book has been cataloged by the Library of Congress
under ISBN 978-1-4813-0848-9.

To Lev
1937–2009
giving thanks with a grateful heart

Contents

Acknowledgments

This book would not exist without the support and encouragement of my children, Lev Prichard IV and Peggy Prichard Fagan, who read multiple drafts and never asked me to change or delete anything. I could not have written this without their blessings.

At Baylor University, Robert Darden, professor in the department of journalism, public relations, and new media, and his wife, Mary, believed in my book from the beginning and gave me both the confidence and professional support necessary to complete the manuscript and see it to publication. They read and edited early drafts, taught me how to write a book proposal, and guided me through the search for a publisher. As mentors, editors, and friends, their involvement was indispensable.

Helen Harris, grief expert at the Diana R. Garland School of Social Work, Baylor, taught me the language of grief and recovery. Throughout my years of writing, she remained available to read and edit sections where precise language and terminology were essential. The Baylor University Libraries allowed me to access databases that otherwise would not have been available to me. Special thanks to Kathy Hillman and Carol Schuetz.

My professional advisors read, critiqued, and edited relevant parts of the manuscript, strengthening chapters on financial and legal issues. I am especially indebted to Sol Schwartz, Trey Tune, Kerri Mast, Thomas Davis, and Jeffrey Myers. Throughout the process, they have been encouragers.

Beverly Thomason and Mary Ann Tanner served as my spiritual mentors, sharing their wisdom gleaned from years of widowhood; they were always available to meet when I needed clearer heads than mine to work through and write about difficult personal issues.

With experience in ministry and in publishing, Gary and Debra Klingsporn provided counsel and direction during countless porch times on Nantucket and gave me the opportunity to lead a series of conversations on moving from loss to joy.

My cousin Susan Wise Bauer—historian, educator, and author—was always ready to share wise advice from her years' experience in the publishing world and offer a calming and reassuring word.

The sisterhood shared their stories with me and permitted me to share them here. They know who they are. This is their story, too. How blessed I am to call them friends.

Thanks are due to Carey Newman, Director of Baylor University Press, and to Cade Jarrell, Jenny Hunt, Diane Smith, Aaron Cobbs, Madeline Wieters, and David Aycock. I am also grateful to my publicist, Kelly Hughes.

On the home front, Sharon Hengen and Raquel Salinas kept my office and household functioning so that I could focus on writing. Without them, I could never have found the time to write this book.

My thanks to all of you. You made this possible. It takes a village.

A Letter to My Fellow Widows

Nothing prepared me for widowhood. As my husband's health began to fail, I knew that his early death was likely. Congestive heart failure, if not quite so predictable as cancer, is a terminal disease. I began to pay more attention to business and financial issues, and—out of necessity—I took on some of the chores that had always been on Lev's "honey-do" list. Nevertheless, I felt completely unequipped for his death and all that had to be done in the aftermath.

Bank accounts, his office and business, the new car he bought just four days before his death, filing for probate, taxes—the list of his responsibilities, which one day were his and the next mine, went on and on. Our adult children were in shock. Despite their dad's long hospitalization, they thought everything was okay when he came home from the hospital a month before his death. Overwhelmed by their own grief, Lev IV and Peggy could not comfort me. As mom, my immediate task was to comfort them.

When the family began to work with our attorney, accountant, and banker, we realized that all the years of estate planning had focused on taxes. At every meeting, Lev's attorney assured me, "Nothing will change when Lev dies." *Everything changed.* How could it not change? This was April 7, 2009, in the midst of the Great Recession, one month from the bottom of the stock market. I was a week away from Tax Day but knew nothing about income tax preparation. Assets were pouring out the door, and I could do absolutely nothing to stop the bleeding.

That first month I was completely overwhelmed. I had amnesia. I still cannot remember much that was said and done. I lived in a fog. I misplaced everything I set down, including Lev's wallet with his identity inside. There were days when I crawled back in bed and pulled the covers over my head. I had panic attacks. My heart raced and I could not swallow. Worry kept me from sleeping. For months afterwards, I repeatedly overreacted out of stress, fear, and exhaustion. Tensions developed with my advisors and my children. I was living a nightmare.

Searching for the eye of the storm that swirled around me, in desperation I turned to prayer and Scripture. Again and again, I read the Apostle Paul's letter to the poor, discouraged congregation at Philippi—a letter full of love, encouragement, and joy. It became my primer for widowhood. I prayed one prayer, which I still pray: *Lord, give me wisdom and discernment and help me protect the family unit.*

I looked for role models and mentors. I recalled family stories. I listened to the stories of other widows. I sought the advice of professionals in the field. I read widely and deeply. From all of these, I slowly gathered wisdom, as well as the confidence to believe that life could be good again. In trying to make sense of my experience, I wrote—tweets, emails, letters, Facebook posts, essays. Out of all the writing, the thought of a book emerged—a survival guide of sorts—to help other widows navigate through grief.

Practical advice from Paul's letter to the Philippians is the thread that stitches my vignettes together, but this is not intended to be a religious book that adheres to any narrow creed. Occasionally I have been explicit about my faith experience; but for the most part, faith is implicit in my story of moving through grief to acceptance and ultimately to joy.

Explore the pages of this primer in whatever way you find helpful, wherever you are in your journey. You can read it through in a day or two. Use it as a daily meditation guide, creating a quiet space in your day to nourish your soul; or check the table of contents to find a chapter that addresses what is on your heart at that moment.

My advice to others, when they lose a spouse, is to listen to your heart and listen to your body. This is a time when you are emotionally and physically fragile. You will not be able to avoid every uncomfortable task; but when you have a choice, choose what is rewarding and fulfilling, not what depletes you. What works for one person does not necessarily work for another. Your circumstances may be very different from mine. Write your own script.

I hope that by writing openly and honestly about my own journey and sharing what I have learned along the way, I will help you to see that you are not alone. You are not the first woman to start on this journey. You will emerge from the overwhelming cloud of grief. Life is not over. Make the years ahead good ones.

Wishing you grace, peace, and joy,
Ella Wall Prichard

The Valley of the Shadow
of Death

In the month after Lev's death, I found comfort reading the Apostle Paul's letter to the Philippians, along with the Psalms and the Gospel of John. In those quiet moments, I found a peace that I could not find anywhere else.

I would like to claim that my adult life has always included formal daily prayer and meditation, but it has not. I fear I use God too often as a celestial bellhop, calling in my orders only when my human efforts fail. I am no mystic; but in times of great stress and deep anxiety, I turn to Christian meditation—a blending of Western faith traditions with Eastern techniques. On those rare occasions, I experience the profound presence and peace of God.

I first practiced meditation in about 1976. My mother gave me a copy of the recently published New English Bible, a British translation; and I was captivated by the elegance of the language. I read the New Testament chapter by chapter, and in about forty days I reached Mark 11:22–24.

> Have faith in God. I tell you this: if anyone says to this mountain, "Be lifted from your place and hurled into the sea", and has no inward doubts, but believes that what he says is happening, it will be done for him. I tell you, then, whatever

you ask for in prayer, believe that you have received it and it
will be yours.

The changes in verb tenses in that translation—*is happen-
ing . . . you have received it*—made all the difference to me. I
learned to pray with thanksgiving rather than anxiety, claim-
ing God's promise that He would do what He had promised.
After a year of thanking God daily for what He was doing, I
saw my prayer answered in a very visible, public way.

God went back to being my bellhop—there for me when my
parents died in the eighties—until September 1995, when Lev's
mother, Helen, was diagnosed with an inoperable brain cancer.
A month later I fell while crossing the street and broke my foot.
I was confined to a cast and wheelchair through the Holidays.
A fog of depression settled over our house. I announced that I
was canceling Christmas. When Lev came home each evening
from the office, he reminded me of the cartoon character Joe
Btfsplk, Li'l Abner's friend and jinx, who always walked around
Dogpatch with a dark cloud looming over his head. Lev's grief
was contagious. I sank deeper and deeper into depression.

When my cast was finally removed and I could walk and
drive again, I went to the bookstore and searched the shelves
of the self-help section. I bought every book on meditation
that I could find. Each morning after Lev went to work, I sat at
my desk, working my way through the Psalms, the Gospel of
John, and Philippians. I journaled for the first time. I prayed.
To prepare myself for the gloom that would reenter the house
when Lev returned, I went downstairs to our shadowy living
room late each afternoon, assumed the classic lotus position of
yoga, and practiced deep breathing with "Je-sus" as my mantra,
while my mind conjured up images of peace and serenity. The
Twenty-Third Psalm took on new meaning:

The Lord is my shepherd; I shall not want.
He maketh me to lie down in green pastures: he leadeth me
     beside the still waters.
He restoreth my soul:
he leadeth me in the paths of righteousness for his name's sake.

As I meditated, I was transposed from a spiritual desert to a green oasis, where I could rest and where my soul was nourished. I visualized the small lake at the Broadmoor Hotel in Colorado Springs, surrounded by the green grass of the golf course. Cheyenne Mountain was reflected in the water, the silence broken by the music of the carillon wafting down from the Will Rogers Shrine of the Sun. There, in memory, my soul still finds peace.

Helen died in March, and less than a month later our daughter, Peggy, gave birth to her first daughter. Joy replaced gloom, and God slipped back into His role as bellhop. We had four marvelous grandchildren. Times were good, and we built a new one-story house. But slowly, almost imperceptibly, heart and lung disease began to weaken Lev. He was the eternal optimist and fighter, never acknowledging the prognosis, going to the office every day. We continued to travel right up to September 2008.

On New Year's morning 2009, I called 911, Lev was admitted to the hospital, and the final battle began. One evening he had a Code Blue. ICU was full of pneumonia patients, so there was no bed there for him. The kind young hospitalist on duty advised me to spend the night in his hospital room. Alone in the room with Lev, I was inexplicably at peace. I knew, as surely as if I had seen a spirit walk through the door, that God had sent His Comforter to us.[1]

As I reclined in the big chair beside Lev's bed listening to the sounds of his breathing, the words of the Twenty-Third Psalm again flitted into my consciousness. This time, though, different verses spoke to my heart:

> Yea, though I walk through the valley of the shadow of death, I will fear no evil:
> for thou art with me; thy rod and thy staff they comfort me.
> Thou preparest a table before me in the presence of mine enemies:
> thou anointest my head with oil; my cup runneth over.

I knew then with calm certainty that we were entering the valley of the shadow of death and that God had sent the

Comforter to walk beside us on this journey. I had always interpreted King David's psalm to refer to his own near-death encounters. Now it spoke to me too: I would walk through this valley with Lev, but I would come out the other end without him. His journey took him to a different place. I would be irreversibly changed, but I had a sure confidence that I would survive. Today I can say with David:

> Surely goodness and mercy shall follow me all the days of my life:
> and I will dwell in the house of the Lord forever. (KJV)

Love Overcomes Fear

1

Grace

Paul and Timothy, servants of Christ Jesus, To all the saints in Christ Jesus who are in Philippi, with the bishops and deacons: Grace to you and peace from God our Father and the Lord Jesus Christ.

Philippians 1:1, 2

Grace and peace. In the face of death, both sounded like impossibilities. My friend Alice was right when she warned me, "They will not give you time to grieve." In fact, I welcomed the busyness, for I did not want time to think: not about the pain of the recent past with Lev's declining health and final illness, not about all the business that needed to be taken care of immediately, and not about the possibility of living decades as a widow. I discovered that if I worked at my desk until I was too tired to hold my head up any longer, I could fall asleep without being flooded with too many bad memories from the past or fears about the future.

My fear and anxiety overwhelmed me. Mustering the courage and will to plow ahead consumed my energy. Trying to grasp my legal and financial situation overloaded my brain. One week after Lev died, I was walking across the library after lunch when I received an unexpected call from his financial advisors—three people sitting around a speaker phone in Chicago. I was given no forewarning, no opportunity to have Lev's attorney on the line. Quite the opposite. They wanted to have an unfiltered conversation without him. The team leader informed me that the bank (one of the too-big-to-fail banks, reacting to the financial catastrophe that was in high gear by April 2009) would no longer manage my investments as it had for generations of Lev's family. I was given thirty days to decide whether to give the bank total discretion for all investments, including asset allocation, or manage them myself.

I became hysterical. Shaking, I screamed into the phone, "You hypocrites . . . coming to Lev's funeral when you knew about this! He must be rolling over in his grave." I slammed the receiver down. Taking a deep breath to gain some control, I called Lev's attorney. He, too, was furious.

In subsequent conversations with the bankers, he reminded them of their fiduciary obligations and negotiated six months for our family to find new advisors. The bank agreed to resign immediately as cotrustee and coexecutor of Lev's estate, leaving me bereft.

Through the years, Lev repeatedly told me that I did not need to know his business because "they will be here for you." They were not. He said, "Everything you need is in the four-drawer locked file cabinet." It was not. In quick order, the family met with Lev's attorney and accountant to begin the whole big process of filing for probate, settling the estate, and finding new financial advisors. I summoned the courage to tackle Lev's office.

Since 1975 Lev and Ralph—his partner, mentor, and friend-like-a-brother—had occupied office space on the same floor in a downtown bank building. When Ralph retired from active involvement in their small, independent oil and gas company, Lev reduced the size of his office. After their longtime secretary died, he relied on an answering machine and an accountant who officed one floor up. He worked with the decorator, filling his new space with furniture and mementoes from his family, including his grandfather's big desk. This was his space.

I made the same daily trip that he enjoyed so much each day: picking up mail at the downtown post office, a haven for the homeless, and then to the parking garage, service stairs, crosswalk to his building, elevator to sixth floor, and down a long hall to Suite 600. I felt like an intruder searching through his space. I dreaded what I might find when I opened a drawer or a file. I dared not throw away a scrap of paper without examining it first. I had no cause, no suspicion to think he might have lived some secret life; but still I feared the unknown. This was work I had to do alone.

Lev was a man who cleared his desk every night. In all our years of marriage, I never picked up so much as a sock off the floor. On the surface, everything appeared normal. There, in the right-hand desk drawer, were the papers he had gathered for our tax returns. The file room, however, told the story of the declining health that he tried to hide from me. I could date his decline by the state of his files. Three four-drawer file cabinets were overflowing. Shelves built to hold office supplies were piled with monthly reports dating back several years. All of it was paper that I had to sift through.

Because I was still in a fog of grief, barely able to function, my daughter, Peggy, stepped in to arrange an interview with an independent personal assistant who worked for several of my friends. We hired Sharon, and she learned the company's filing and bookkeeping system from the accountant upstairs. Scott, my son-in-law, recommended an oil and gas attorney, who scoured all the legal papers to learn the business in order to teach me what I had to do. My son, Lev IV, went with me to the insurance agency to review all the insurance policies. They turned out to be in as much disarray as the papers in the file room. I moved the *Wall Street Journal* to home delivery, and it became my financial textbook. I labored over the *Journal* every day, with Barron's *Finance & Investment Handbook*—all 1,220 pages—at my side so that I could look up every unfamiliar word, acronym, and phrase. I was terrified by my responsibilities. Lev had taken very good care of us.

His longtime bank trust officer—retired by then—wrote me: "Lev always impressed me with the top priorities in his life: the church, his family, and leaving his family more than he inherited. . . . After thirty-six years of administering trusts, I can count on one hand the number of customers who more than tripled their inheritance, over a lifetime, for their heirs. It is almost impossible to do, given the temptations to spend and to expand one's lifestyle. And Lev did it while also being very generous to his church and to charity."

Now it was my turn, and I was not equipped.

Five years later, a financial advisor who met me shortly after Lev's death wrote, "During your married life you were in some ways the stereotypical spouse who was either excluded from financial decisions or who sat quietly during the meetings. The knock on such spouses is that they are woefully unprepared for the responsibility of leading the family after dad's passing. Some even take for granted that the widow must be inadequate given the husband's decision to treat them this way. I think even some of the widows take this for granted! Not so, in your case. You made the choice to step into those shoes and worked hard to make sure you did it well. You brought certain gifts to the challenge, but many aspects of it were daunting and required extraordinary effort."

I never considered myself a needy person, but now I needed so much: to surround myself with advisors whom I trusted; to learn to ask for help; to lay aside my pride and admit that I did not understand; to extend and receive grace. I surrendered privacy, regularly copying information to all my advisors and my family. Lev IV said, "Mom, you're confused." Scott said, "Ella, I think maybe . . ." I needed them both. I needed Peggy and my daughter-in law, Cheri . . . the grandchildren . . . friends. In the loss of that most significant relationship, I needed to nurture the relationships I still had, while reaching out and building new relationships.

With all that confronted me, I still did not take time to mourn. Though I sometimes thought I was losing my mind, I never considered a grief recovery group.

Later, several friends who joined groups told me that the regular sharing of memories and experiences with others who understood was invaluable, while others reported that their group "stayed at the pity party" instead of moving forward. Some found the approach too formulaic—Steps 1-2-3 toward recovery—when in reality, every widow's grief is unique.

I asked Dr. Helen Harris, grief expert and assistant professor at Baylor University, Waco, Texas, if she recommended grief recovery groups. Harris insisted that there is no right answer. Some benefit from being in a group where their feelings are normalized, while others can get caught up in others' grief and feel worse instead of better. She advised, "If it makes you feel better, stay with it. If it doesn't, stop and try something else."[1]

Reflecting back on that period, I believe that if I had addressed my grief head-on in the beginning instead of numbing myself with busyness, I might have healed more quickly. Where did I get the idea that I must not break down . . . that I needed to be strong . . . that I needed closure?

I identified with the poet Edward Hirsch, who described his own overwhelming grief after the loss of his son in a NPR interview. Discussing his book-length elegy, *Gabriel: A Poem*, Hirsch said, ". . . poetry takes courage because you have to face things and you try to articulate how you feel. I don't like the whole language of healing which seems to me so false. As soon as something happens to us in America everyone begins talking about healing, but before you heal you have to mourn and I found that poetry doesn't shield you from grief, but it does give you an expression of that grief. And trying to express it, trying to articulate it gave me something to do with my grief."[2]

My journey was not smooth or easy. Progress was not steady. Repeatedly, I stepped unknowingly into sinkholes, those undetected emotional triggers that ignited my anger or grief or depression.

The novelist Joyce Carol Oates named them in her memoir, *A Widow's Story*: "The widow must learn: beware sinkholes! The terror of the sinkhole is that you fail to see it, each time you fail to see it, you don't realize you have blundered into the sinkhole until it's too late and you are being pulled down, down. . . ."[3]

My reaction to those sinkholes jeopardized my relationships with my professional advisors and even with my children. Thankfully, ours was a close, loving family. We quickly realized that our unity was essential and that the family came first. We learned to extend grace to one another—to forgive one another for words spoken in frustration, anxiety, or grief. As we grew to trust one another in our new roles and relationships, my anxiety lessened. Slowly, I relaxed. Eventually, I was able to find peace in my new situation. It took me fifteen months to begin to see daylight, another year to have a firm grip on my finances. More than four years later, I was finally ready to process my grief through writing about it—not with Hirsch's elegant, moving poetry, but with prosaic vignettes of death, grief, rebuilding my life, and reclaiming joy. Now I know that this journey never ends. I am still a work in progress.

❀

Lesson learned: Grace is the bottomless well of God's unconditional love, mercy, forgiveness, and pardon. It is the gift of unmerited favor. Those of us who receive His grace are bound to extend the same grace to others. And in the giving and receiving of grace, we find inner peace and peace with others.

2

Gratitude

I thank my God every time I remember you, constantly praying with joy in every one of my prayers for all of you, because of your sharing in the gospel from the first day until now. I am confident of this, that the one who began a good work among you will bring it to completion by the day of Jesus Christ. It is right for me to think this way about all of you, because you hold me in your heart, for all of you share in God's grace with me, both in my imprisonment and in the defense and confirmation of the gospel. For God is my witness, how I long for all of you with the compassion of Christ Jesus.

Philippians 1:3–8

When Ralph got the call about Lev's death, he said, "Ella is going to find out how easy Lev made her life." He was right, but that discovery did not lead to gratitude. Instead, I was angry and overwhelmed. *Lev, where are you? I'm not supposed to have to do this!* Income tax? Insurance? Medicare forms? Car, house, and yard maintenance? Bills, budgeting, banking? Lawyers and accountants? I had no experience with any of that. I went from my parents' home to my husband's home, where I was privileged to be a stay-at-home mom.

I still find myself overwhelmed and bewildered by a flat tire or a dead battery. I am still irritated when I need to have the car serviced or washed. I have friends who have never written a check or pumped their own gas; who have never carried their own suitcase, traveled, or dined out alone. A few have never spent a night apart from their husbands except in childbirth. Many, like me, resisted their husbands' efforts to explain family finances.

As I struggled during those early months of widowhood, Sol, Lev's longtime accountant and friend, advised me, "Ella, you haven't climbed this mountain before, so it's difficult. Take it one step at a time. Eventually, you'll get to the top and it's downhill from there."

As a child, I loved the little story of *The Little Engine That Could*,[1] the Little Blue Engine that huffed and puffed up the mountain—"I think I can, I think I can, I think I can"—so that the good boys and girls on the other side would have toys to play with and good food to eat. So every morning I got up muttering, "I think I can, I think I can, I think I can," as I put one foot in front of the other and tackled the tasks before me.

Remembering my friend Betty's example of "living life in gratitude mode," one of the tenets of Al-Anon, the twelve-step program for families of alcoholics, I began to count my blessings. To start with, I was of reasonably sound mind and body. I was financially secure. I had caring friends and loving, responsible children. I had faith. Since I usually was home alone for lunch—just a quick break from my desk—I claimed that as a time to pause and pray, "Thank you, God, for . . ." I started focusing on the forty-six years that Lev and I had, his provision for us, the blessings of family. I thanked God for all those other people in my life who were supporting me at this crucial time. I thanked Him for the coincidences (were some of them acts of Providence?) that made my life—or my day—or my hour—better. I even learned to say "thank you" for the setbacks that taught me important lessons.

The words of the Apostle Paul to the Philippians—his beloved congregation—became my words about Lev: *I thank God every time I think of you. I recall our time together with joy. I remember that everything I have is the result of your hard work.*

One thing I'm certain of: that you are well and whole again in the presence of the Lord. Though I miss you now, I know that I shall see you again. That expectation with thanksgiving brought me comfort and peace.

I was gratified to know that Lev had enough confidence in me to entrust me with his business and his estate. I could have chosen dependency on my children and advisors, but I felt that I honored him and his wishes by accepting responsibility. That created one small problem. Lev and I both led full, busy lives. I had happily embraced the philosophy adopted by Ralph and his wife, Jean—that if they worked in separate spheres, they would together know and accomplish twice as much. Now, I paid for my ignorance.

How would I maintain my identity and continue to do the things that brought me joy while taking on all of Lev's work? I feared becoming a drudge, a drone.

I never guessed that Helen, my mother-in-law, would become my role model for widowhood. Lev's dad was killed in a plane crash when Lev was only thirteen and his mother, thirty-nine. About eighteen months later Helen married Russell, and for more than twenty years they enjoyed the good life together. Then, in her early sixties, she was widowed again. I recalled her announcement shortly after Russell's death:

> "I am going to accept invitations to go out. At first you don't feel like seeing people, and so you turn down invitations. People want to be kind; but if you keep saying 'no,' they will soon forget you and move on. Then when you're ready to be with friends again, they're not there for you."

Joyce Carol Oates made a similar decision. In an interview for *Publishers Weekly*, she said, "If I don't say yes [to every offer] I am going to go down a deep hole and never get up."

Carrie Tuhy wrote about Oates, "She accepted invitations to travel, to see movies, have dinner and give lectures and readings—things she would never have agreed to were Ray alive. 'Nineteen out of 20 things turned out well,' she says, and at one dinner party, she met Charlie Gross. They eloped soon after."[2]

When I was half a couple, I could say, "I don't feel like doing that." After Lev's death, I emulated Helen and tried to say "yes" to everything. I knew that if I lived reactively, only responding to the invitations that came my way, simply acceding to others' plans, I would find myself among the widows who sat home alone at night. I became proactive in planning times with others. As half a couple, I could say at six o'clock, "I don't feel like cooking. Let's go out." As a new widow, I had no friends—married or single—whom I was comfortable calling at the last minute. Many friends and even casual acquaintances were kind and invited me out after Lev died. I quickly realized that I not only needed to reciprocate but also to initiate social occasions if I wanted to be invited a second time.

Lev and I routinely threw away invitations to civic and charity events. After his death, I seriously considered and often accepted such invitations, even attending large functions by myself. We made charitable contributions to organizations we believed in. As a widow, I began to factor in the social and networking opportunities that were among the perks of support. I was often uneasy and uncomfortable in my new role. I did not know how to initiate conversations with strangers. Alone, I struggled to walk up to a group. I pushed myself far out of my comfort zone.

I was already dreading the Holidays, more than seven months away. Genevieve Davis Ginsburg, a social worker and widow, described the plight of the new widow in her helpful book, *Widow to Widow*:

> Special occasions . . . are not easily thrown away like yesterday's garbage. They are dates to be reckoned with. Most of us acknowledge that we are sad, mad and depressed and feel very sorry for ourselves at such times—perhaps for a whole week before the actual date. But we also count it a milestone when we survive that day for the first time. The second time is less foreboding.

For the newly widowed, the days from Thanksgiving until New Year's could easily be turned in for scrap. . . .

. . . All the seasonal goodwill and the well-intentioned people looking for needy recipients on whom they can lavish that goodwill are small comfort to her. She would much rather be sitting next to her husband on the holiday looking around for *their* lonely person.

Nothing works and everything hurts. Participating in the holiday dinner of former friends is a lonely affair. Being taken in by the cheerful congregation is definitely patronizing. . . .

The fact is we really don't want to be part of someone else's tradition.[3]

Having always loved everything about Christmas— the tree, carols, presents, cards, cookies, candies, and lavish meals—I did not want to lose that too. How could I move from loss and grief to the joy of Christmas? I set goals for myself, borrowing literally from the word *thanksgiving*. I resolved to focus on giving thanks. I planned a large, early-evening open house before Thanksgiving as a way to thank all those who had been kind to me after Lev died. The invitation was properly formal and subdued, the party properly sedate and decorous.

At the same time I planned my Thanksgiving party, I designed my Holiday card. Since 1967, the year Lev IV was born, we had sent Christmas photo cards. Every major life event was marked in that year's card. My list grew to several hundred as friends moved away and we stayed in touch through the annual card exchange. I was not ready to say, "Merry Christmas!" and I did not want to receive cards addressed to "Mr. and Mrs." Not everyone knew that Lev had died. What to do?

In my church, we sang a little praise song, "Give thanks with a grateful heart."[4] I often hummed the melody as I worked around the house. That became the theme of my Thanksgiving card—a montage of photos that told the story of Lev's life from the time he was a baby through our marriage and children to the grandchildren and the family trips, all the happy memories for which I continued to give thanks. The only clues of his death on the card were the dates, March 4, 1937–April 7, 2009, under his name and the closing, "Wishing you a blessed Thanksgiving, Ella." I mailed them in mid-November; and by the time Thanksgiving came, I was ready to face the Holidays.

The idea of being alone on major holidays, even for an evening, still terrifies me. I cannot have what I want most, which is to have Lev alive and all the children and grandchildren gathered around my tree and my table. I struggle to be thankful for what I have, instead of wishing for a past that cannot be. While I seldom fall into sinkholes any longer, I sometimes stumble and trip on the rough spots in the road. Each year is better. I have become more proactive and less dependent on my family in planning my holidays. I am learning how to celebrate fully and joyfully without Lev.

❀

Lesson learned: In our despair, we cannot imagine that life will ever be good again. By living in gratitude mode—counting our blessings, continually saying thanks—we can move from despair to confidence. We can find joy in our memories of the past and our anticipation of the future.

3

Insight

And this is my prayer, that your love may overflow more and more with knowledge and full insight to help you to determine what is best, so that in the day of Christ you may be pure and blameless, having produced the harvest of righteousness that comes through Jesus Christ for the glory and praise of God.
Philippians 1:9–11

My younger friend went through her home screaming, "I am not a good Christian woman! I can't do this!" She had just brought her husband home from the hospital after yet another serious heart procedure. She was coming to grips with his declining health and her potential role as caregiver. I assured her that we all feel this way.

On the worst days, I wondered, *Is this the first day of the rest of my life?* This was part of the guilt and regret that I carried after Lev's death, but I learned through friends who had been there before me that it is normal. Most of us unconsciously crossed our fingers when we said our wedding vows to be faithful "for better or worse, for richer or poorer, in sickness and health." Few would marry if we thought our future would be worse, poorer, or full of sickness. Young love breeds hope and brings joy. The reality is much more complex.

While finding hope and joy again was the furthest thing from my mind in the aftermath of Lev's death, I drew from the spiritual virtues and disciplines cultivated by a lifetime in the church to find the emotional resources to move forward. My family needed a strong bond of love to hold us together at a time of unprecedented grief and anxiety. I needed both information and insight to make decisions that would be best for all of us.

I recalled a lesson that I had learned in the 1970s, which served me well as a new widow. At a time when I was devoting most of my waking hours to a significant community project, I justified it to my minster by explaining that I had been reared to do my best always. He asked me one simple question: "Ella, is it worthy of your best?"

What required my best now? How did I establish priorities? What demanded my immediate attention? What could I postpone or delegate to someone else? Whom could I trust? Knowing the difference between right and wrong was not enough. I needed to distinguish among good, better, and best.[1]

What I came to think of as "Lev work" was all-consuming. I had a business to manage, an estate to settle, advisors to hire, and bills to pay. All that required my best. I had little time for my "Ella work," which really was not work at all: quality time with family and friends, volunteer work, travel, and entertaining.

From the time I read the Apostle Paul's advice to the poor, quarreling, discouraged Philippians, I began to pray that prayer that would become my mantra: *Lord, give me wisdom and discernment and help me protect the family unit.*

Beverly, one of my two spiritual mentors, was one of the wisest women I have ever known. I first met her when she was teaching a women's class in the young married Sunday School department that I attended in the early 1970s. Beverly, who grew up in the small West Texas town of Breckenridge, enrolled in Baylor University in 1943, when the only male students were either unfit for military service or studying for the ministry. Her senior year she noticed Johnny, a good-looking returning veteran. To her delight, he enrolled in the noncredit typing class she taught. Back in Breckenridge for the Christmas holidays, she received a package from him—an apple wrapped in foil Christmas-tree icicles. They started dating in January, became engaged in April, and married in August 1947, when he graduated.

Throughout their sixty-one years of marriage, they lived in Corpus Christi, where Johnny was a Realtor. They served faithfully in church leadership positions for decades while rearing three sons. No matter what her personal difficulties were, Beverly never faltered.

She was in her eighties when Johnny died, but she continued to display serene confidence. She accepted her season of life with grace and dignity. Using a cane, she traveled to New Zealand and the Czech Republic, knowing that she could not participate in every activity but rejoicing that she could visit places that she had long dreamed of seeing.

After Lev died, she gave me invaluable advice: "Ella, you need to give yourself permission to do things differently than Lev would have. What worked for him may not work for you." She described how lonely she was in her big, two-story house after Johnny died. Trying to maintain the yard and keep the grass watered in drought conditions overwhelmed her. She installed a sprinkler system, something Johnny never wanted. Soon afterwards, she put her house up for sale and moved to an independent living facility where many of her friends lived.

Lev IV and Peggy did not want change. Though they were especially attentive, loving, and caring to me after their dad's death, they had their own families and work that demanded their attention. They struggled with the idea of my stepping into Lev's shoes, making all the changes that I thought were necessary in the wake of his death.

Peggy wanted her relationship with me to remain unchanged—for me still to be the mom she had always known, not someone with whom she had to do business. Lev IV hated change in principle, and he had difficulty accepting all the changes thrust upon us. I had always embraced change, and now I wanted to make changes immediately so I could mark them off the list and "get it over with." I did not know then what I realize now: that adjusting to the death of one's spouse is never completely "over with."

I wanted to empty Lev's closet quickly, in order to turn his bedroom into a home office and close the downtown office, which I despised. I canceled his post office box. I moved and closed bank accounts. I sold his Ford Thunderbird. I bought a condo in Dallas. And that was just the beginning.

Lev's empty chair illustrated the family's differences as we worked our way through grief. When friends came to call after they learned of his death, my children clenched their fists as other people unknowingly sat in their dad's chair. When our family of nine was alone in the library, they squeezed as two family groups into the pair of flanking couches, leaving Lev's chair empty. I, on the other hand, could not bear the empty chairs or the empty bed.

There was the empty chair opposite mine in the library, where we drank coffee and read the newspaper together each morning and watched the news before dinner each evening. There was the empty chair across from me in the breakfast room; another, at the head of the long dining room table. There was the big armchair in the living room, his chair since 1971. There was the empty bed where he died.

Some turn those empty places into shrines, memorials to their spouses. That is not my nature. My mind overflowed with memories, and sometimes I needed to escape them. Within a few months, I bought a pair of chairs for the library and claimed for myself the space his chair had occupied. In the breakfast room, I did a ninety-degree turn, to face out the French doors to a flower-filled patio instead of across the table to the empty chair. In the dining room, I moved to the chair at the head of the table, symbolic of my assumption of the role as head of the family. In the living room, I opted for lighter-weight chairs, which could be easily moved for an intimate visit with a handful of friends, instead of the large circle of heavy furniture appropriate for a half-dozen couples.

Lev's bedroom became my new office and his closet, my file room. French doors opened to a tiny porch, where I added attractive outdoor furniture, a small bronze statue, and new landscaping. His newly purchased desk went where the bed had been, facing the porch; but everything else stayed in place. On impulse, I made one unplanned addition. I moved his old library chair into the office, on the other side of my desk, where I saw it every day when I worked there. Oddly, in that room where I assumed a new role overseeing the family businesses and taking care of the "Lev work," I found comfort in the reminders of his presence.

Six years later, I asked my decorator if other widowed clients also redecorated.

"Always!" Ann replied. One client could not bear to look at the chair her husband had spent so much time in when he was dying of cancer. The memories were too painful. Several of her clients moved within a few months, seeking a new home without memories. When I asked her about the universal advice to wait a year before making any major decision, Ann was emphatic. "I totally disagree." With a smile, she added, "There's also a guilty pleasure in being able to do it just the way you want." We laughed as we recalled painting the bedroom walls green—a color Lev hated—in my new condo.

I never realized all Lev did each day at the office to make my life so easy. Now I was responsible for his work. While I never became proficient at handling paper once—something Lev did effortlessly—I was forced to become better organized, keeping my new home office strictly for business to satisfy the IRS. I started sorting the mail in the library. Business mail went to the office and personal mail to my old desk in my bedroom, while magazines and travel brochures landed on the coffee table. Junk mail was tossed instantly into the trash.

In the years since Lev's death, the division between "Lev work" and "Ella work" has grown wider. Even after I dissolved the partnership with Ralph and turned over Lev's other business interests to outside managers, when I no longer had to maintain a business/personal dividing line for the IRS, I found that I preferred writing notes, sending birthday cards, and dealing with other personal correspondence at my personal desk. I could not write this book in the office. I needed separate space for my "Ella work."

By trial and error, I acquired clearer insight and better judgment about making changes. The rate of change slowed. I took longer to reflect before I acted. I weighed my decisions more carefully. For the most part, I figured out whom to inform and consult about what—family, friends, advisors. The "Lev work"—bills, cars, and household maintenance, as well as legal, accounting, and financial issues—became mostly routine and predictable. When I grew weary of a task, I could lift my eyes from the paperwork or the computer screen and soak in the beautiful, quiet space of the office and the green space beyond it, feeling a sense of accomplishment that I did what had to be done. While I did not choose and do not want this role, I gradually grew accustomed to it. I obtained some balance in my life, finding time again for the people and the activities that had always brought me pleasure. I found a degree of contentment.

❀

Lesson learned: Love, coupled with wisdom, discernment, and insight, leads to good decisions and healthier relationships.

4

Courage

I want you to know, beloved, that what has happened to me has actually helped to spread the gospel, so that it has become known throughout the whole imperial guard and to everyone else that my imprisonment is for Christ; and most of the brothers and sisters, having been made confident in the Lord by my imprisonment, dare to speak the word with greater boldness and without fear. Some proclaim Christ from envy and rivalry, but others from goodwill. These proclaim Christ out of love, knowing that I have been put here for the defense of the gospel; the others proclaim Christ out of selfish ambition, not sincerely but intending to increase my suffering in my imprisonment. What does it matter? Just this, that Christ is proclaimed in every way, whether out of false motives or true; and in that I rejoice.

Philippians 1:12–18a

Courage without fear? How terribly frightened and anxious I was about the task before me—not only settling the estate and stepping into Lev's shoes to assume oversight of his various business interests but also the prospect of living alone and making a life for myself for years to come. Only one grandparent died before age 90. My dad's mother lived beyond 100, as did her father and her oldest daughter, Adeline, who lived to 106.

Daddy's family furnished contrasting models for aging. When he was fifty, Papa Wall—my grandfather—announced to the family at the dinner table that this might be his last Christmas with them. When he retired from the railroad fifteen years later, he sat in his chair and waited for the Lord to take him. While his mind and eyesight slowly failed, he patiently waited twenty-nine more years. He had always petted on and cared for my grandmother, who was ten years younger than he. When he died, Daddy and his siblings worried about who would take care of her. They needn't have. Mama Wall lived another nineteen years, her mind intact until the end. As a child, I found her mean and self-centered; but as an adult, I grew to respect her feistiness and determination, which battled all constraints. She did not surrender to physical infirmities. I was convinced then—and am convinced now—that she did as well as she did for so long because she never passively accepted her fate. (My mother—her daughter-in-law—had a different opinion. She said that Mama Wall was so ornery that God didn't want her.)

And then there was Adeline, my most admired aunt and role model. Born in the rural South in 1899, her life spanned the entire twentieth century. With scant education but a sharp mind, she married as a teenager and bore two children. Only thirty-seven when she was widowed, she educated her children and then moved to Tallulah, a small town in northeast Louisiana, where she bought a small, white frame house and opened a women's clothing store with her younger sister Jessie. She became an integral part of her new community. An excellent cook, Adeline frequently entertained friends at her home, which she had furnished with antiques bought in New Orleans. She took painting lessons in her spare time and became an accomplished artist. Nothing seemed beyond her grasp once she set her mind to do it. My mother said of Adeline and her siblings, "Walls have will power." I too was a Wall. I was determined to display the same degree of will power.

Adeline and Jessie, the most affluent members of the family, opened their shop partly to generate income for their parents after retirement; and for many decades they were in their shop virtually every day. With token support from their brothers and sisters, they provided for Mama Wall for more than thirty years.

As a teen, I rode the bus to Tallulah every summer to visit for a few days, going to work with them each morning. At the end of my stay, I always returned home with a suitcase full of new clothes. When I graduated from high school, Adeline and Jessie gave me a long, white, strapless, tulle ball gown for my senior prom. When I became engaged, they asked me to meet them at the Dallas apparel market, where I bought my wedding dress and trousseau at cost. In every way they were encouragers. Of all the relatives on both sides of my family, they were the ones who routinely detoured through Texarkana, where my family lived, when they traveled. They came to my wedding in Texarkana and to my graduation from Baylor University in Waco, Texas. They drove across two states to Corpus Christi to attend my parents' fiftieth wedding anniversary and to visit Daddy when he was dying of cancer. They returned when he died, and they made the trip again to visit Mama.

Adeline outlived her parents, seven siblings, and only son. She outlived her car and drove across the Mississippi River bridge to Vicksburg to buy a new one when she was in her nineties. She continued to live alone in her home, half a continent away from her only daughter, until she was almost one hundred. Finally, she moved to a retirement home in Seattle. Lev and I visited her about a year before her death. Her daughter arranged lunch for us in a small private dining room at the home. Using her walker, Adeline walked erectly into the room, her white hair freshly styled. She could no longer speak, but she immediately recognized me and wept as she attempted to greet me.

When I returned home after her graveside service in Magnolia, Arkansas—where she had married and reared her children and where her husband was buried—I asked Peggy, "Can you imagine being a widow for sixty-five years?"

Peggy, then thirty-five, responded, "I can't imagine being married sixty-five years!" And, of course, few of us are. Given the longevity in my family, I could be a widow for more than thirty years—a truly frightening prospect.

How, then, to move from fear to courage—something Adeline appeared to do so effortlessly—and ultimately to reclaim joy? I needed to figure that out. To reclaim joy with the degree of resilience, generosity, and sheer grit that Adeline consistently displayed was yet another challenge.

When I was growing up, Daddy frequently instructed me, "Do what you have to do first. That way you can fully enjoy your remaining time doing what you want to do without that nagging reminder in the back of your mind." After Lev died, I instinctively sought to work as hard as I could for as long as I could in order to plow through the tasks in front of me, to climb that mountain of grief.

While Daddy's advice got me through probate, I discovered that the work was never completely done and I could never revert to my old role. I struggled to maintain a healthy balance between the "Lev work" and the "Ella work," to take care of myself, and to be around the kind of people and involved in the kind of projects that I found fulfilling and satisfying. I tried to avoid critical, negative people, as well as organizations that were full of stress and conflict. In short, I needed insight, as well as the courage to act on that insight.

My income did not stretch as far as it did when Lev was alive, so I had to pick my charities more carefully. I discovered the quintessential American virtue of enlightened self-interest: that in doing for others and in involving myself in activities that bettered the community, the church, and the world, I benefited most of all.[1]

My motivation was not as pure as Lev's. He quietly supported the church, education, and institutions that improved the quality of life in our community. He had a heart for institutionalized children, and he knew how to lend a hand to others without being patronizing. After his death, I supported causes that provided opportunities for me to spend time with people I liked and admired. I invested my time in organizations that brought me pleasure. I expanded my community to Dallas, Nantucket, and Colonial Williamsburg. In each community I enjoyed the benefits of support that Lev never sought from nonprofit institutions.

At the same time, I continued to work my way up the mountain at an unrelenting pace. However, I soon realized that God had good reasons for creating the seventh day for rest. I learned how to balance work and leisure, time alone and time with friends and family, time at home with old memories and time traveling to create new memories.

For years I wanted to be a change agent. I loved the challenge. When I was in high school, I stumbled upon "A Psalm of Life" by Henry Wadsworth Longfellow. I can still see the double page in my mind's eye—Longfellow's poem superimposed on a black-and-white photograph of a deserted beach with footprints in the sand. I have never forgotten the words of the seventh stanza. They have always motivated me to make a difference:

> Lives of great men all remind us
> We can make our lives sublime,
> And, departing, leave behind us
> Footprints on the sands of time;

At this point in my journey, I was finally weary of change. I still supported change in theory, but I no longer wanted to fight for it. I no longer could fritter away my time in activities that were not personally fulfilling. I no longer felt obligated to cram my life with good works. I wanted to spend whatever time, talent, and treasure I had left on what mattered most to me. Relationships. Relationships. Relationships.

New York Times columnist David Brooks focused on moral character when he began an important national conversation in his 2015 book, *The Road to Character*. He wrote that the book was the product of his own spiritual journey—his search to identify the character traits that really mattered and to figure out how those traits were developed. One of the traits he examined was courage. Like Longfellow, he recognized what is required to make a difference in the world we live in.

Brooks described Mount Holyoke College at the beginning of the last century: "A dozen voices from across the institution told students that while those who lead flat and unremarkable lives may avoid struggle, that large parts of the most worthy lives are spent upon the rack, testing moral courage and facing opposition and ridicule, and that those who pursue struggle end up being happier than those who pursue pleasure." Students were urged to absorb the heroism of the ancient Greeks and Romans—"to be courageous and unflinching in the face of the worst the world could throw at you."[2]

Brooks' final words are excellent advice for those of us who grieve:

> Each struggle leaves a residue. A person who has gone through these struggles seems more substantial and deep. And by a magic alchemy these victories turn weakness into joy. The stumbler doesn't aim for joy. Joy is a byproduct experienced by people who are aiming for something else. But it comes.
>
> There's joy in a life filled with interdependence with others, in a life filled with gratitude, reverence, and admiration. There's joy in freely chosen obedience to people, ideas, and commitments greater than oneself. There's joy in that feeling of acceptance, the knowledge that though you don't deserve their love, others do love you; they have admitted you into their lives. There's an aesthetic joy we feel in morally good action, which makes all other joys seem paltry and easy to forsake. . . .
>
> Joy is not produced because others praise you. Joy emanates unbidden and unforced. Joy comes as a gift when you least expect it. At those fleeting moments you know why

you were put here and what truth you serve. You may not feel giddy at those moments, you may not hear the orchestra's delirious swell or see flashes of crimson and gold, but you will feel a satisfaction, a silence, a peace—a hush. Those moments are the blessings and the signs of a beautiful life.[3]

The new widow needs courage simply to get out of bed, to go to a party alone, to celebrate the family's major life events without her husband beside her. Every small act of courage empowers us. Those small acts, repeated often enough, give us the confidence to build new, meaningful lives for ourselves. Paired with wisdom and insight, courage leads us to accept our changed circumstances with grace and serenity. Courage is an essential early step toward reclaiming joy.

As I examined and repurposed my life in the years after Lev's death, I began to experience moments of giddy exhilaration and sheer joy and even brief periods of settled happiness.

❁

Lesson learned: Widows who faced life alone without fear, courageously overcame obstacles, found joy even in times of crisis, and lived purposefully and contentedly serve as role models and mentors for those of us who follow them.

5

Expectations

Yes, and I will continue to rejoice, for I know that through your prayers and the help of the Spirit of Jesus Christ this will turn out for my deliverance. It is my eager expectation and hope that I will not be put to shame in any way, but that by my speaking with all boldness, Christ will be exalted now as always in my body, whether by life or by death.

Philippians 1:18b–20

At dinner one night Janet said, "All the joy went out of my life when Jack died." The other three of us nodded in agreement. We had all been there.

I raised my glass and paraphrased the toast offered at my rehearsal dinner so many decades earlier: "To health, wealth, and happiness . . . and friends to enjoy them with."[1]

Say it again. *Rejoice!* What an impossible admonition. On top of the grief, those first months after Lev died were consumed by the drudgery of learning the business and settling the estate. Joy was not even on the horizon. A psychiatrist might say that avoiding painful memories and frightening possibilities was repression, but I found that controlling where my mind wandered was essential to my emotional survival. I threw myself into a frenzy of activity, collapsing into bed so exhausted each night that I fell asleep with relative ease.

Lev IV and Peggy probably thought I grieved too little. In their distinctively different ways, they struggled with their grief for months. Nevertheless, their lives returned to normal. They were back in their own homes with their families intact. Their lives had a rhythm that was only interrupted for a short while. On the other hand, everything changed overnight for me, and my life would never be the same again. I did not know until six years later that there is a word for this—*bereavement.* It literally means "to have been robbed." While I mourned the loss of Lev, I also mourned the loss of marriage and companionship, as well as the life I had lived as half a couple, as the wife of a successful man. I did not cry. I felt a desperate need for self-control. If I lost control, if I started crying, I might never stop.

Grief memoirs were too painful to read while I was still grieving; but when I read them years later, I recognized myself. Joan Didion, in particular, captured in words much of what my first months were like:

> Grief turns out to be a place none of us know until we reach it. We anticipate (we know) that someone close to us could die, but we do not look beyond the few days or weeks that immediately follow. . . . We imagine that the moment to most severely test us will be the funeral, after which this hypothetical healing will take place. When we anticipate the funeral we wonder about failing to "get through it," rise to the occasion, exhibit the "strength" that invariably gets mentioned as the correct response to death. . . . We have no way of knowing that the funeral itself will be an anodyne, a kind of narcotic regression in which we are wrapped in the care of others and the gravity and meaning of the occasion. Nor can we know ahead of the fact (and here lies the heart of the difference between grief as we imagine it and grief as it is) the unending absence that follows, the void, the very opposite of meaning, the relentless succession of moments during which we will confront the experience of meaningless itself.[2]

I had choices. I could wallow in self-pity, sink into depression, and let family and advisors take charge of my life and my affairs. I could simply react to whatever came my way. Or I could take charge of my future. I could not change the fact of Lev's death or the terms of his will. I could not change the economic realities of 2009. I could not change the fact that I was a widow. However, I could choose to defy the stereotypes of widowhood and embrace the years that lay in front of me. I could—most of the time—control my thoughts.

During the course of his long career, Walter Mischel, psychology professor at Columbia University, studied and wrote about the mastery of self-control. His advice? "It's to keep living in a way one wants to live and work, to distract [from grief or other melancholy thoughts] constructively; to distract in ways that are in themselves satisfying; to do things that are intrinsically gratifying."[3]

Carol Dweck, Stanford University psychology professor and Mischel's former student, took his research a step further in exploring the significance of a person's mindset. She observed that the view we adopt for ourselves influences the way we live our lives. If we have a growth mindset—if we believe that we can change—we are more likely to change.[4]

I did not have to look far to find women whose circumstances were far more difficult than mine, yet they had risen above circumstances to live full, rich, productive, happy lives. As I had so many times before in the fifty years I have known her, I looked to Mary Ann M., who—with her husband, John—lovingly and tenderly reared a daughter who was mentally challenged. Mary Ann and John started dating in high school and married while they were students at Baylor. When I met them in 1963, John was working on the family farm and Mary Ann had resigned her teaching position to care for Carolyn, their new baby girl. They were already serving in leadership positions in our church and the community.

In the early years of our friendship, Mary Ann took a blind woman in our church on an outing every week. When I asked her why, she explained, "Whenever I start feeling sorry for myself, I look for someone in a worse situation than mine and

I do something for them." That kind of continual thoughtfulness and kindness marked her life.

I remembered Mary Ann's prayers when she and John struggled to accept the reality of Carolyn's limitations. Her prayers guided me when Lev died. "First we prayed that it wasn't so," Mary Ann recalled. "When we recognized the reality of her situation, we prayed for a miracle. When we realized there would be no miracle, we prayed that we would live our lives in a way that would be a blessing and encouragement to others."

She and John blessed others for decades as they encouraged other parents who faced similar challenges. They gave their time and resources not only to assist the institutions that housed Carolyn, but also the Corpus Christi State School, which housed those dependent on government assistance. Mary Ann's life was a testimony that constructive distraction works. Serving others can take our minds off our own tough circumstances.

I wanted to be a testimony, too—an encourager to other widows and a role model for future generations of widows in my family. I felt the strong and certain presence of the Comforter from that January night in the hospital with Lev through his death and burial. Now I claimed God's promise, *We know that God causes all things to work together for good for those who love God, who are called according to His purpose* (Rom 8:28). The only way I could think of to bring good from the sad circumstances of Lev's death was to live my life with the faith, courage, hope, and expectation that I professed to believe. I found that I could do that only by living life in community, with the love, support, and prayers of others.

Kay was another of my role models. She was only forty-three when Phil, a minister, died of cancer. Their son was in college; their daughter, still at home. A former teacher who had served beside her husband in ministry, Kay had to go back to work. A local church called her as children's minister. She had just moved to a new position in another city when she was diagnosed with leukemia.

In 2014, her sister summarized Kay's life as a widow in a Facebook post:

> Fifteen years ago today Kay's husband Phil passed away. It has been a really tough journey for Kay but she has taken the challenges and passed with flying colors. For my friends who don't know Kay, she is my baby sister. In the time since Phil's death she has made three career changes, conquered leukemia (almost eight years) and received a graduate degree in social work. To say Kay is a survivor is a HUGE understatement. Phil would not be surprised but would be so proud of the woman she is today.

Some years ago, Kay posted a meme: *When life gives you lemons, throw them back and demand chocolate.* I was ready to settle for lemonade, but Kay taught me to expect more. I want chocolate. My goal is to live as a widow so that life includes all the richness and sweetness of dessert.

According to Elaine M. Brody, a pioneer gerontologist, expectations play a huge role in our happiness. When she was eighty-six, she presented her final scholarly paper, "On Being Very, Very Old: An Insider's Perspective." What she said about being old applies to widows as well. She raised the question, "Is it good to be very, very old?" She could have easily asked, "Is it good to be a widow?" And then Brody answered her own question. "IT DEPENDS. And it depends on our expectations." She described her friend Betty's welcoming speech at her ninety-eighth birthday party, "I'm glad you are all here, and I'm glad I'm here, too."

"Remember," Brody wrote, "she is 'exceptional, not typical.' She has enough money, has a very pleasant living style, is essentially in good health, has good functional capacity, has a boyfriend, and has plenty of beautiful clothes. (That last variable does not appear on any morale scale.) Her lifestyle meets her expectations."[5]

While that sounds superficial—how many ninety-eight-year-olds have a boyfriend?—I have friends whose lives do not measure up to what they expected. Failing health and financial reversals can lead to bitter disappointment. Expectations need to be realistic. Have we saved enough to maintain our desired lifestyle? Have we taken good care of ourselves? Are we in good shape—physically, mentally, spiritually, and socially?

Life is not over. We need to take a personal inventory. What changes do we need to make in our lifestyle? We may not be able to recover financially, but we can learn to live gracefully within our means. Our doctors can advise us on the steps we can take to be healthier. We can stay actively engaged socially, intellectually, and spiritually. We can reclaim joy.

❀

Lesson learned: If our expectations are realistic and our hopes are grounded in faith, we can find contentment and purpose—even joy—in our new role.

6

Joy

For to me, living is Christ and dying is gain. If I am to live in the flesh, that means fruitful labor for me; and I do not know which I prefer. I am hard pressed between the two: my desire is to depart and be with Christ, for that is far better; but to remain in the flesh is more necessary for you. Since I am convinced of this, I know that I will remain and continue with all of you for your progress and joy in faith, so that I may share abundantly in your boasting in Christ Jesus when I come to you again.

Philippians 1:21–26

I do not see death as gain. I choose life. I had an overwhelming amount of work to do after Lev died. My family needed me, and my time with family—especially the grandchildren—was where I found my one bit of joy. Several friends confided that, like me, they lived in denial of the possibility of widowhood, rejecting their husbands' attempts to teach them the basics of their finances. One expressed the firm hope that she would die before her husband or—even better—that they would die together.

Though traumatic events and natural disasters wipe out entire families from time to time, they are extraordinary exceptions to the norm. The reality is different: by their early sixties women outnumber men in the U.S. population, and by age seventy-eight the majority of American women are widows.

Women who were sixty-five in 2012 can expect to live another twenty and one-half years, while men the same age can expect almost eighteen more years.[1]

Consider U.S. Census data. The 2014 American Community Survey estimated that there were almost twenty-five million women over age sixty-five but fewer than twenty million men. Seventy-two percent of the men but only about 46 percent of the women were married. About 11 percent of American men were widowed but more than 35 percent of women.[2]

The logic is inescapable: Most women marry older men, and men tend not to live as long as women. Most of us will be widows.

So there I was, unprepared for all that I must do, immediately confronted with practical and legal realities. Overnight, I moved from the role of smiling spouse and gracious hostess to that of executor, trustee, CEO, and—most dreaded of all—matriarch. I am not sure that anyone had confidence in me. I certainly had none in myself.

Because I faced a six-month deadline to replace the bank—not only as investment managers and financial advisors, but also as cotrustee for the estate—we began the long search almost immediately. I could not have done it alone; Lev, Cheri, Peggy, Scott, Lev's attorney, and his accountant were all involved. When we interviewed prospective advisors, one particularly pompous candidate kept referring to "the matriarch." I did not know to whom he was referring, but then it finally dawned on me: he was referring to me! *Matriarch* was barely a word in my vocabulary, certainly not a role to which I had aspired or for which I had rehearsed. It took me more than four years to comprehend all that the role encompasses. In summer 2013 I wrote my children:

> Not every widow is a matriarch. Sometimes, the role of head of the family passes from father to a child, usually the oldest son, because the widow lacks leadership, independence,

self-confidence, and initiative. She shifts her dependence from her husband to her children. That wasn't something I was ready to do, and I don't think it would have been fair to you all if I had added to your responsibilities at this place in your lives. Now that I've finally figured out the job description, I guess I can spend the rest of my life trying to meet the qualifications for the position—especially the last two points. It's really a pretty daunting task. I'm lucky to have you all to help me. So thanks.

The role of a matriarch is:

- To protect, preserve, and—if at all possible—grow the estate;
- To protect, preserve, promote, and pass on family history, values, and traditions to the next generations;
- To protect, preserve, and promote family harmony;
- To step proactively into the role of titular head of the family through personal leadership, initiative, moral authority, self-confidence, and independence;
- To live her life consistent with the values and character traits she hopes to pass on to the next generations;
- And, by the grace of God, to do all the above with love, respect, kindness, affection, affirmation, generosity, fairness, integrity, transparency, and gratitude.

Critical estate issues consumed my time for more than a year, and most family conversations and get-togethers revolved around business. We needed time for the nine of us simply to enjoy ourselves together. In summer 2010 we met in Venice for a week-long cruise around the boot of Italy to Rome, with time during the day for everyone to pursue individual interests, then time each evening for us to gather and celebrate family.

I envied friends who were able to organize big family vacations each year. But with four hundred miles between Lev's and Peggy's families, Lev IV's unpredictable schedule as an airline pilot, and age and gender differences among the grandchildren, finding a time and place that worked for everyone was increasingly complicated as the grandchildren grew older and reached adulthood. I understood that my role was to facilitate but not to dictate quality family time, though there was sometimes a disconnect between what I understood and what I wanted—another sinkhole.

I remembered a sermon I heard almost ten years earlier. When George came to Corpus Christi as senior minister at our church, I identified with him as a peer. We overlapped as students at Baylor, and we had many mutual friends. He was also one of the most dynamic preachers that I have ever heard—a real stem-winder. Therefore, one Sunday when he described how he liked to be right, to have the last word, and to win the argument, I paid attention. He described me, too.

Then he added, "But I have learned with age that it is more important to be rightly related than to be right."

That sentence resonated with me. Protecting relationships is far more important than winning arguments. I try to think before I open my mouth to demand or criticize or offer unsolicited advice. *Is this worth risking the relationship?* Almost always the answer is "no."

None of us had any idea how drastically Lev's death would impact the family dynamic. That loss left a huge hole that was impossible to fill. *Someone is missing!* Living every day with that black hole, I longed for family time to fill the void and to fill the house with joy and laughter again. I suspected that the family avoided my house because of the void. I attempted to be strong, to hide my yearnings and my hurt, and to accept the realities of my children's crowded and complicated lives. I did not want to burden them with my loneliness; but on the occasional days when I was overwhelmed by the silence and the emptiness, my pain spilled out—usually on Peggy, who lived nearby.

For five years I tried to live with the black hole. I tried to accept the fact that no one could replace Lev as my confidant.

I thought I was strong enough to bury my emotional need for someone to whom I could bare my soul. I finally acknowledged the impossibility and instinctively turned to Peggy for emotional support.

What I thought was a uniquely personal response to my loss turns out to be the norm. Most married women consider their husbands their main confidant. When they are widowed, their daughters usually assume that role. Elaine M. Brody spent decades studying the relationship between mothers and daughters, which she analyzed in her groundbreaking book, *Women in the Middle: Their Parent Care Years*:

> *Emotional support* is the most universal form of family caregiving, the one most wanted by older people from their children and the one the adult children themselves feel is the most important service they can give their disabled parent(s). It is also the kind of help for which no government or paid worker can substitute. The provision of emotional support cannot be quantified and is probably underestimated with respect to the time and effort consumed. Its importance to the elderly cannot be overestimated. It includes being the confidant or the one with whom problems can be talked over; providing social contacts such as phoning, visiting, or taking the elderly person out to family events; and help with decision-making. Most of all, such support means giving the older person the sense of having someone on whom to rely—someone who is interested and concerned, who cares, and who listens.[3]

Daughters almost always have this responsibility; almost all of them feel stress, many suffer from depression, and 75 percent feel guilt that somehow they are not doing enough, that they cannot make their mothers happy. I did not want Peggy to be a statistic. I did not expect her to make me a higher priority than her husband and children. Neither she nor anyone else could make me happy. But I did depend on Peggy in myriad ways, and life would be much emptier if she and her family did not live in the same city.

A childless, widowed friend often reminded me, "You have a wonderful family"—another reason for gratitude. Widows without children must be far more strategic than I in planning for advanced old age. Those whom I know are superb friends. They take beautiful care of one another, but they worry about their future.

Despite a loving family, I worried about my future, too. I had been robbed of the most significant person in my life. Every holiday, every major life event where Lev was absent was a new robbery, new bereavement. The losses kept coming, and none of us were prepared for them. Nobody warned us that death was only the first loss. When I did not fall apart immediately after Lev's death or at his memorial service, my family and friends thought I was strong. When I repeatedly fell into sinkholes for months—and occasionally, for years—afterwards, everyone was surprised. The children did not know how to react or what to do when I plunged into depression and self-pity.

Alan Keith-Lucas, in his classic book *Giving and Taking Help*,[4] wrote that everyone who experiences loss experiences shock and denial and protest—the sense of being robbed. However, not everyone goes on to mastery of her grief.

Dr. Helen Harris described how some "detach and despair and never fully recover." The goal to "be strong" can contribute to this if the bereaved person is denying her feelings and natural responses. The degree of protest is directly related to the degree of mastery.

"Oh, I protested," I told Dr. Harris. "I ranted on Twitter and Facebook." I knew that protest was permissible. The Psalms are full of David's protests to God. Jesus, as he was dying on the cross, *cried with a loud voice . . . "My God, My God, why have you forsaken me?"* (Matt 27:46). What I did not know was that protest is mentally healthy and leads to recovery.

Until this point in my journey, I rejected the idea that full recovery was ever really possible. However, if I accepted Dr. Harris' definition of recovery—which seems close to Keith-Lucas' theory about mastery—then recovery was an achievable goal. She explained: "Recovery is the place where we are managing our grief instead of it managing us and our responses. Some people think that recovery means that we are fine, as if it never happened. I don't believe that ever happens. I don't believe the best answer is to 'let go.' Instead, I believe that we integrate the life and death of our loved ones into the total picture of our lives. Recovery is perhaps that place where we remember without reliving the experience of loss."[5]

Ever so slowly, I became more open with the family about my emotional needs, fears, and anxieties. When we began to communicate more honestly, we found our way back to the family we were before Lev died, able to enjoy one another without the constant intrusion of family business. With clearer understanding and more realistic expectations, I began to relax. I shifted my focus from myself and my grief to my family and friends. I reclaimed joy when I reached the point of acceptance, contentment, and hope. Finally, I could look forward to Christmas with anticipation.

❀

Lesson learned: When we quit focusing on our own loss and begin to focus on the needs of others, when meeting their needs becomes more important to us than our personal desires, we will find meaning and purpose for our lives. We open ourselves to joy.

7

Unity

Only, live your life in a manner worthy of the gospel of Christ,
so that, whether I come and see you or am absent and hear
about you, I will know that you are standing firm in one spirit,
striving side by side with one mind for the faith of the gospel,
and are in no way intimidated by your opponents. For them
this is evidence of their destruction, but of your salvation. And
this is God's doing. For he has graciously granted you the priv-
ilege not only of believing in Christ, but of suffering for him as
well—since you are having the same struggle that you saw I
had and now hear that I still have.

Philippians 1:27–30

One older friend complained that she had to obtain permission from her son and trustee to buy a new dress. An
elderly relative confided that she blithely traveled the world
while her son/trustee managed her affairs, until one day he
said, "Mother, there is no more money." Media accounts told
the sad, sordid story of New York socialite Brooke Astor, who
lived to age 105. Her 89-year-old son was found guilty of stealing $185 million from her during the years he had fiduciary
obligations as her trustee.

The word *fiduciary* is not in most people's vocabulary. A
few weeks after Lev died, the family met with our attorney
and accountant. They reviewed the terms of his will and trust,
explained how the terms would affect us, and outlined all that
I needed to do as executor and trustee. Because Lev's bank had

resigned, I did not have the professional assistance that Lev and I had always taken for granted. At the end of the meeting, Cheri said to Lev IV, "I don't know what *fiduciary* means, but it sounds important. I think we need to find out."

In the simplest terms, a fiduciary or trustee has three legal obligations:

1. The duty of care: to pay attention, to read the reports, to act responsibly;
2. The duty of loyalty: to put the best interests of the trust and its beneficiaries first, ahead of any self-interest;
3. The duty of obedience: to honor the terms of the legal documents and applicable state and federal laws.

In recent years, many attorneys promoted the creation of marital and family trusts, even for middle-income couples. Some friends, including those with modest savings, put all their assets—including their homes—in trusts while both were alive. Trusts have many values, but they also have a downside. As one widowed friend said, "I know we have to have trusts. That doesn't mean I have to like them."

First, most trusts seem to be based on the assumption that the surviving partner will be a dependent little old lady who needs to be taken care of. She loses privacy and autonomy, perhaps the most offensive aspect of trusts for most widows.

Second, the flip side of preserving the estate and protecting it from creditors, divorce settlements, and spendthrift heirs is that trusts tie up capital. The beneficiary—the widowed—often has strict limitations on tapping the principal of the trust.

Third, estate planning is largely driven by the goal to reduce taxes. I could not remember a meeting in forty-six years of marriage where professional advisors discussed with us the difficulty of administration or the stresses on the family. Certainly, they did not tell us what we would pay them in fees to execute what had been designed during those many years.

While a particular trust may be the best way to protect family assets from undue taxes, the potential psychological costs to beneficiaries need to be considered as well.

Fourth, irrevocable trusts such as marital and family trusts are exactly that. Circumstances and tax laws may change, but one can seldom go back and undo the trust once it is created. The survivors—the beneficiaries—are usually stuck with the consequences. We cannot foresee the future. The terms of a trust drafted when times are good may be onerous by the time the trust goes into effect. What works for an intact family may not work so well after a divorce. Generations die out of order.

My new attorney assures me that "it doesn't have to be that way"; but by the time we become widows, it is usually too late for us to make significant changes.

Growing up in a thoroughly middle-class family, I had no knowledge of trusts and other estate-planning documents when I married Lev; but about three months later, we found ourselves in a Chicago courtroom suing his grandmother. I was nauseous. At age sixty-five and dying from cancer, Lev's grandfather—an Oklahoma wildcatter who built a large, independent oil company—wrote his will and established trusts. He left part of the estate in trust for his only son, the principal to be distributed to him at age forty-five. One year later, at age forty-two, Lev's dad died in a plane crash. According to the terms of the trust, Lev, thirteen at the time, was to receive the income of the trust after his twenty-fifth birthday. Until then, his grandmother would benefit. But Grandmother, who was about eighty and bedridden, was not ready to relinquish her extra income when Lev turned twenty-five. The bank's trust department could not transfer payments until the court ruled on the issue. While Lev's relationship with his grandmother remained good and she seemed quite pleased with his choice of me, relations among members of the extended family were permanently poisoned.

Trusts can change everything. Most importantly, they can change family relationships. A widowed mother and her children become primary and remainder beneficiaries, with built-in conflicts of interest. Simply put, the more a widow spends, the less the children inherit. A single word buried in a trust document can make an enormous difference in the widow's access to principal.

Even when they are not trustees, heirs have the legal right to be informed about the status of the trusts. Achieving unity—having a shared vision of how funds are to be managed and distributed—is challenging and requires great intentionality. Unity does not happen by chance. Family members have different personalities and needs. They respond differently to stress. They grieve differently.

Today the trend is to designate a family member as trustee instead of a bank trust department. However, having a corporate trustee has one significant advantage: trust departments are Switzerland. They are neutral, intent on administering the trust fairly, according to the legal language in the document. This avoids the conflicts of interest and mistrust that can develop when one beneficiary is also trustee.

In the first quarter 2016 *Women and Wealth Magazine* article, "Crossed Wires: Why Most Generational Wealth Transfers Fail," Scott Clemons cited a twenty-five-year study of wealth transfers,[1] which found that 70 percent of transfers failed, with just a tiny percentage due to poor professional advice. A staggering 97 percent of failures were due to the breakdown of family communication and trust.

My responsibilities terrified me, but I was determined to protect both the family and the estate. I had no practical how-to books to guide me and few friends who had climbed this mountain ahead of me. My advisors did not furnish me with a written checklist for settling the estate. Instead, they gave verbal instructions, one step at a time. In my eagerness to "get it over with," I leapt ahead of them. I made mistakes, especially in disposing of Lev's personal effects.

Due to inadequate information, I was persuaded to renounce my community property rights, which were protected by Texas law. Discovering my mistake—fortunately, before I had signed a legally binding agreement—I was furious with Lev's attorney. I sent out a brief, blunt email to the family and advisors, notifying them that I had changed my mind.

While I did not need Lev IV's and Peggy's permission legally, I desperately wanted their approval of my job performance and their blessings for my big decisions. I was hurt when word drifted back of conversations with the words, "What are we going to do about Mom?" I interpreted their questions and opinions to suggest that I was somehow dishonest or selfish or greedy. In my pain, I lashed out and accused them of the same. My failure to discuss the situation with them privately—before I sent out instructions to my advisors—created a painful, difficult situation. We all had to extend a lot of grace to one another and to forgive one another. It took a long time for all the wounds to heal.

In spite of those early misunderstandings, I could always count on my children's support when I encountered significant challenges from the outside. For six months they and their spouses were by my side for twelve interviews with prospective financial advisors, traveling to four cities in three states. When my name, as executrix, replaced Lev's as defendant in a nuisance lawsuit, Lev IV completely lifted that burden from me by working with Lev's real estate attorney to prepare for trial if necessary and to negotiate an acceptable settlement if possible. As my suspicions grew that Lev's attorney was not adequately representing me, Lev IV and Peggy backed me up.

Gradually, I built my own team with the family's active involvement: first, a new financial advisor and trust officer; then, a new attorney; and finally, after our accountant's retirement, a relationship with a younger partner in his firm. My new advisors related to me very differently than those who originally knew me as Lev's wife. As one of them told me, "You own us."

In several steps over several years, I shed the day-to-day management of Lev's businesses. On the advice of my advisors and with the approval of my family, I dissolved his long-time partnership with Ralph, auctioned off remaining operating interests, and turned over management of Apco Minerals to the oil and gas division of a large regional bank. I finally trusted my new financial advisors enough to give them discretion in investments.

As a family, we grew to accept the full authority of what Lev had put in writing. In some cases, we had to ignore what he had told us in private conversations. We resigned ourselves to the fact that his estate plan was what it was and that we had to live and work and relate to one another within its parameters. Lev IV and Peggy began to trust my judgment. With their help, I finally reached the top of the mountain that I had struggled so long and hard to climb.

When I rewrote my will about nine months after Lev's death, I asked Lev's attorney to explain it line by line in boring detail with my children present. Later, with my new attorney, I made additional revisions. I emphasized: *ease of administration and elimination of every possible conflict within the family after my death are more important than lowering taxes.*

My effort to maintain family unity was not a one-time undertaking. It was ongoing. If I wanted my family to trust my leadership, I needed to consistently exhibit unconditional love, transparency, honesty, fairness, and generosity. While I chafed at first at what felt like a loss of privacy and autonomy, I grew to appreciate my advisors' counsel. They worked with many families in our circumstances. Their broad experience was invaluable when I needed help in navigating difficult issues. Knowing my own limitations, I counted on them to keep me both legal and solvent.

I want to leave my affairs in good enough order that Lev IV, Peggy, and the grandchildren will not be unduly burdened by administrative responsibilities in settling my estate. I want them to have the kind of professional services that I expected but did not have. I cannot completely protect them from being responsible for my care if I live to advanced old age, but I have made it clear to them—and I have put it in writing—that they have my permission to arrange for the best care for me when I am not of sound mind or body, regardless of what I might say or how I might act at that time.

From time to time, my attorney and I revisit my will, medical power of attorney, and other legal documents, tweaking them where we can, trying to ensure that Lev IV's and Peggy's climbs up that mountain will not be as difficult as mine was. Thank God we are unified. I trust that the pieces are in place to protect family unity for years to come.

❀

Lesson learned: Family unity is essential to successfully navigate the treacherous waters of settling, managing, and dividing an estate. Therefore, strengthening family bonds should be a top priority for every new widow.

Unity Strengthens Relationships

8

Encouragement

If then there is any encouragement in Christ, any consolation from love, any sharing in the Spirit, any compassion and sympathy, make my joy complete: be of the same mind, having the same love, being in full accord and of one mind.

Philippians 2:1, 2

When his mother, Helen, died of brain cancer in 1996, Lev, her only child, was devastated. Bill, her third husband, eight years older than she, had significant health issues of his own. In those last months of her life, they had separate round-the-clock caregivers. During the twenty years of their marriage, we grew close to Bill, his sons, and their families. We loved having a big family with a grandfather, uncles, aunts, and cousins for our children.

However, at the end of Helen's life, we unwittingly made decisions that damaged our relationship with Bill's family. Lev and I literally and figuratively tiptoed around planning her memorial service and—later—disposing of her personal possessions, not intending to keep secrets but rather trying to be sensitive to Bill's frail health. Since 1966 Lev had always been the one who stepped in when a family member died— his grandmother, stepfather, two aunts, and my parents. With medical power of attorney and as his mother's executor and heir, he assumed authority quickly and confidently.

In the midst of our own grief, neither of us realized that we needed to include Bill and his family in the decision-making. We did not know how to involve them. Only later did we sense the hurt that we had inadvertently inflicted. At the very least, we should have communicated with them in advance of any action. Ideally, we should have worked with them to build consensus on end-of-life issues, Helen's service, and the transition that necessarily followed.

From that experience, I learned how very fragile families are in times of grief, especially blended families. While we cared about Bill's health and well-being and genuinely grieved when he died several years later, Helen was unequivocally our first priority. Likewise, while Bill's family loved Helen, their primary concern was Bill's health and how he would cope with Helen's death. Caught up in our separate but overlapping fears and concerns, we failed to encourage and comfort one another. Therefore, we lost the opportunity to build unity and strengthen our relationship.

Second marriages are fraught with opportunities for misunderstanding and conflict. Bill's situation was similar to what widows often experience when their husbands have children by a previous marriage. Adult children sometimes want to take charge. Serious disputes can arise over property and personal effects from a previous marriage.

Nuclear families are not exempt. A large family that I know well still struggled a year after their mother's death. The youngest daughter's eyes filled with tears when she said, "Mother's death should have brought us together. Instead, we're all over the place. Mother would hate this because she was all about family." In their efforts to protect their own individual interests, they ignored their mother's wishes and questioned the terms of her will. "That isn't what she intended," they argued.

Books for young widows include chapters on dealing with the in-laws. In their deep grief, parents are not always prepared to step back graciously when their daughter-in-law plans a service in a different faith tradition or arranges a secular service. And the service is only the beginning. Issues of money, child-rearing, and—later—dating and remarriage often create tension. Some parents smother their daughter-in-law and grandchildren with attention in their hunger to hang on to their son's family. At the other extreme, parents occasionally blame their daughter-in-law for somehow causing their son's death.

When a family has internal discord and conflict, it cannot have the strength and unity needed to fend off external threats. In the aftermath of Lev's death, our family gathered to plan his service with Paul, our former pastor who knew all of us well. Though Lev left no written instructions, we knew intuitively what he would want. We had no disagreements. As we surveyed the long list of all that had to be done immediately, my children and their spouses divided up responsibilities, freeing me to spend time with close friends who called to offer comfort.

Reflecting on that period several years later, I marveled that Lev IV and Peggy went about their tasks so calmly and efficiently. Their grief was enormous. I leaned on them for emotional support while they turned to me for comfort, as they had when they were children. Their spouses, Cheri and Scott, were rocks. They loved Lev but were detached enough to encourage me, comfort their spouses and children, run errands, answer the phone and the door, and in general keep us all functioning.

A week after the service, I was back at home, alone, trying to understand all that had happened and all that I needed to do. At our first family meeting, our advisors shared their experiences from decades of advising families going through probate: families function best when there is transparency and openness—no secrets or surprises. They alarmed us when they described how frequently family members sue one another over estates.

We were all determined not to let that happen in our family. We knew that Lev's heart would be broken if he thought the family was fighting. Respect for his memory and our shared love for him and for one another was all the encouragement that we needed to stay focused on family unity. Because we were emotionally fragile, we all overstepped at one time or another. We were all changed by our grief, and we needed time to learn to relate to one another in these new circumstances.

Through the years I have heard the warning, "Be careful how you treat your children because they will pick your nursing home." I hungered for my children's blessings, their approval, and—most of all—their presence. I needed to feel needed, and that surprised them. Peggy said later, "I never thought of you as a needy person." I wanted them to read my mind, to know what I wanted and needed without my having to ask. I did not want to nag, whine, or beg. Emotionally, I needed to know that they wanted to be with me. I wanted it to be their idea, for I did not want them to feel obligated to see me or to do for me. When I did not hear from them, I felt rejected, forgotten, unwanted, unloved. Alone.

Like most older women, I never want my children to be responsible for my physical needs. I do not want to be dependent, but I do depend on them, and I will most likely have to depend on them more as I grow older. I know that while they are the center of my universe, I am not the center of theirs, though that universal truth is far easier for the head to grasp than for the heart. The best gift that I can give my children is to be as self-sufficient as possible now in order to maintain my independence as long as possible. I need to learn to swallow my pride and ask for help when I need it, nurture other relationships, and lay a foundation for my future that will be good for the entire family.

The English clergyman J. B. Phillips, in his 1958 translation of the New Testament, wrote in language that should resonate with every widow but that is equally applicable to other family members:

> Now if you have known anything of Christ's encouragement and of his reassuring love; if you have known something of the fellowship of his Spirit, and of compassion and deep sympathy, do make my joy complete—live together in harmony, live together in love, as though you had only one mind and one spirit between you.[1]

The Apostle Paul did not write that we must agree on every point but that we need to live and work together with a common purpose, in a spirit of love and harmony. Our family discovered that family unity is a noble goal in and of itself, not always achieved. If for no better reason than enlightened self-interest, widows are wise to encourage unity within our families.

Attorney Mark Accettura advised:

> Family is truly the gift that keeps on giving. The family dynamic that you had a hand in creating will survive you, impacting your children and grandchildren. Although many of the events that went into forming your family as it now exists have already occurred, your family is not set in stone. How you live your life from this point forward and how you structure your estate at death are new opportunities to reinforce the healthy aspects of your family, correct past wrongs, and leave a lasting legacy of fairness, compassion and love. . . .
>
> Ideally, as the parent, you should lead in the prevention effort. You are in the best position to create family peace and minimize future fighting. Use your position, perhaps as you never have, to build bridges and mend fences. You may not ultimately be able to undo the old hurts that brought the family to its current state, but you must never stop trying. You can best lead by having your estate affairs in order. Similar to succession planning in business, you need a transition plan and a transition team to implement your vision. Now is the time to take stock of your family portfolio. As the family CEO, you can implement a plan and secure the future course for your family and your assets.[2]

To lose one's husband is painful enough. The thought of losing the entire family through conflict or selfish, controlling behavior is unbearable. When we are healthy and independent, we may not think that we need our children; but those who live to advanced old age will grow increasingly dependent on our families. Our friends will grow old along with us. In most cases, they will not pick our nursing homes.

❀

Lesson learned: If we as widows value our family relationships, we will encourage our family by extending to them the same love, respect, kindness, fairness, and generosity that we want and need.

9

Unselfishness

Do nothing from selfish ambition or conceit, but in humility regard others as better than yourselves. Let each of you look not to your own interests, but to the interests of others.
Philippians 2:3, 4

The loss of a spouse is completely overwhelming. In place of that unique relationship, in place of that companionship, surviving spouses—if they are of sound mind and body and if finances permit—receive an enormous measure of freedom and independence. I call it God's compensation. Like many women my age, I went from my parents' home to my husband's home. Except for a three-month internship at the *Corpus Christi Caller-Times* in the summer of 1962, I never lived alone or supported myself.

Now, as a widow, I could do what I wanted, whenever I wanted, most of the time. There was nobody to tell me "no." I could spend my money as I chose. I did not have to ask permission. I no longer had to consider Lev's tastes. I painted my bedroom green and planted palm trees in the garden, both taboos when I was married. I no longer had to debate which painting to buy, while my choice invariably came in second when I was half a couple.

Still, I missed the feedback. While Lev seldom told me "no," he occasionally said, "You've been smoking those funny little brown cigarettes again," and I knew what he meant. He noticed my purchases, and his simple question—"How much did that cost me?"—served as a yellow caution light. Now, no one noticed or cared when I wore a new outfit.

Lev IV and Peggy did not question my spending, but I did not have complete confidence in my own judgment. Though I always had a separate checking account to cover personal and household expenses, I chose not to know about our total expenditures and financial condition. When Sharon, my assistant, put my expenditures on a spreadsheet after Lev's death, I was shocked.

My circumstances were typical for stay-at-home wives of my generation. In contrast, many younger women are offended by what they consider an allowance bestowed by a patronizing husband, and working wives are far more likely to be equal partners in managing the family finances. Still, many lack full knowledge of their husbands' financial and business dealings. For almost every widow, taking full responsibility for finances, expenses, and investments for the first time is a daunting challenge. Nevertheless, experienced widows and widowers freely acknowledge that they thoroughly enjoy their newfound freedom and independence. For those who were caregivers, this freedom can be especially liberating.

The danger is that the line between freedom and self-centeredness is a very fine one. One friend said, "I've spent all my life doing for my husband and children. Now it's my turn." She had no intention of consulting her children on anything. She made her plans and then told her children what she had decided. I worried about which nursing home her children would pick for her. Another acquaintance lost interest in planning and hosting family gatherings, even on holidays. She turned over all responsibility of fostering family unity to her children.

In contrast, my mother modeled unselfishness, as her grandmother and mother had for her. Her grandfather died in 1878, leaving his widow, Grandma Lucy, with four young children.

Letters at Louisiana State University paint a stark picture of their near-starvation in rural Louisiana after his death.[1] After the family's home was destroyed by a tornado, Grandma Lucy moved to New Orleans, where the three boys—ages twelve, ten, and seven—threw newspapers to support their mother and little sister. Somehow, by 1910 she was financially able to build a two-story frame house in the new Carrollton neighborhood of the city. Mama recalled that her grandmother never turned away a hungry person who came to her door. Remembering that period when her children were hungry and even family members ignored her pleas, she would give her last dollar to a stranger who needed help.

Her youngest son, my grandfather, died in 1942, leaving his widow almost penniless. My grandmother, Mamaw, gave up her home and spent the next twenty-eight years living with her children. Social Security, enacted in 1935, provided her with minimal income, for which she was always grateful to President Franklin Roosevelt. My earliest memory of her was on April 12, 1945. She spent the day in our living room, weeping as she listened to the radio news reports of Roosevelt's death.

Unselfish and nonjudgmental, Mamaw bought Christmas and birthday gifts for all twenty-two of us—her six children, their spouses, and the grandchildren—from her meager income. She made no distinction between her children and the in-laws, treating everyone equally, never interfering or finding fault. We all knew that she loved us unconditionally, and we loved her in return. As a result, ours was a family without drama and arguments. Try as I might, I cannot remember a time when a family member spoke critically about another, not a time when some were on the "outs," not speaking to one another. And no one ever talked about family outside the family.

Many years later, my uncle objected to an essay I wrote about Mamaw, because I described the family as among the "genteel poor." He insisted that they were not poor, that everyone in the South was in the same situation from the Civil War to World War II. But he went on to share a story that illustrated both the family's modest circumstances and unstinting unselfishness. Mama's two older sisters felt the brunt of the family's financial distress. When the two girls went to work after high school, they shared their tiny paychecks with their younger sisters in order to make their teen years better.

Mama absorbed Grandma Lucy's and Mamaw's unselfishness and generosity. When my older brother married, she cited Mamaw as the kind of mother-in-law she intended to be. Mama often did without so that I could "keep up" with my friends and classmates, buying her shoes at a discount store so that I could have nicer ones. Later, I asked her why. "It was more important for you to have nice things," she said. She went back to work when I was in high school so that I could pursue my dream of attending Baylor University. An excellent seamstress, she made all our clothes. I assumed that she loved to sew, but I realized later that she never sewed for herself after I left home. She did all the cooking, washing, ironing, and cleaning, rarely asking me to help. As her mother had done for her and her five siblings, she did for my brother and me.

As a young child, I assumed that all mothers were like Mama. However, as I grew older and spent more time at friends' homes, I noticed that some mothers were self-centered. They wore fine clothes and jewelry and drove expensive cars, while their daughters had less than I did. They expected their children to assume major responsibility for housework, meals, and the care of younger siblings.

Daddy thought that Mama spoiled me, and she probably did. When Lev and I started our family, I worried that Mama's unselfishness might have made me selfish. Would I still want to be on the receiving end, or would I want to give generously— even sacrificially if called on—to my children? Lev IV and Peggy will have to be the judges of whether I measured up.

Of all the intangible gifts that my parents gave me, the great-est was to move five hundred miles from Texarkana to Corpus Christi after Daddy retired. Not only did I suddenly acquire eager babysitters, but they were young enough to make friends and involve themselves in the church and the community. They were not dependent on us for companionship and enter-tainment. When their health failed eight years later (far sooner than any of us expected, given their healthy lifestyles and their parents' longevity), not only was I spared long trips back home to care for them, but their new friends continued to call and visit, lifting some of the responsibility from me.

Every time I watched a friend travel back and forth across the country to check on aging parents or observed one move an elderly, infirm, widowed parent to Corpus Christi, I whispered a prayer: "Thank you, God."

Like everything else in the grief process, the question of when and if to move to the children's location is intensely per-sonal. How do we balance our own desire to be near our friends with the need to make life as easy as possible for our children?

Patricia made the move work. She was sixty-six when she was widowed, sixty-nine when she moved to Houston, where two of her children and their families lived. She had the plea-sure of watching her grandchildren grow up, participating in their activities. Attractive and vivacious, she was young enough to make friends and build a new life in Houston. When she moved, Patricia leased a townhouse in her hometown; and she regularly returned home to see her old friends. She had the best of both worlds.

When we act unselfishly, considering the needs of other family members as well as our own, we lower the risk of fam-ily fights. Sally Kleberg, a member of the famed King Ranch family, wrote:

> In my family, the five members of my grandfather's genera-tion each had their own "money personalities" from carving

out a living from the land before oil was discovered. Later generations seemingly should have similar "money histories." Instead, my fifth generation contemporaries respond to the management of personal finances and the role of the family company in myriad and often highly conflicting ways. Disparate family groups form opportunistic alliances to serve personal perspectives on control, power, and perceived unfairness in divisions of labor and management. If one cousin is in management, another family alliance wants its representative on the board of directors as a counterweight. Personal attitudes of the various factions and individuals toward money in their own lives further complicate the dynamic. Some of them are spendthrifts, others are frugal, depending on their innate money personalities. As the number of minority shareholders in the family company increases, struggles for power and control accelerate at a rate equal to the distance that a family member feels he or she is from effective management and control over the shrinking pot—the pot used to feed the growing number of hungry mouths. There are over 100 of us now; if we don't make an effort to understand the part this plays in our communications, our business meetings can collapse over conflicts.[2]

When I was a child, I was taught in Sunday School that JOY is an acronym for Jesus, Others, You. In other words, to have joy, you need to place God first, then others, and lastly, yourself. That is far too simplistic. We need to take care of ourselves if we are going to take care of others. We cannot ignore our own physical, spiritual, emotional, social, and financial needs; but somehow we must find a healthy balance. If we want a strong relationship with our children, we must respect their other responsibilities and commitments. We need to ask, not demand. And we must communicate openly and honestly.

As Peggy reminded me more than six years after Lev died, "I am a good caregiver . . . when I know what is needed." For too long, I expected her to be a mind reader.

During the years of Lev's declining health and especially after his death, I used up all my emotional resources. My cup was empty. I had nothing more to give. I lost interest in the work of the boards on which I served. I could not muster the energy to provide leadership at my church or even to organize our family Christmas gathering.

However, focusing on my emptiness stripped away all vestiges of contentment and joy. When I took my eyes off myself to reach out to others, I lifted my spirits and nourished my soul. When my spirits were low and I was tempted to throw a pity party, I sang the words of the old hymn as a prayer:

> O soul, are you weary and troubled?
> No light in the darkness you see?
> There's light for a look at the Savior,
> And life more abundant and free.
>
> Turn your eyes upon Jesus,
> Look full in His wonderful face,
> And the things of earth will grow strangely dim,
> In the light of His glory and grace.[3]

❀

Lesson learned: In being more concerned for the welfare of others than for ourselves, we forget our own needs and pain and discover the joy of serving and giving.

10

Humility

Let the same mind be in you that was in Christ Jesus, who, though he was in the form of God, did not regard equality with God as something to be exploited, but emptied himself, taking the form of a slave, being born in human likeness. And being found in human form, he humbled himself and became obedient to the point of death—even death on a cross. Therefore God also highly exalted him and gave him the name that is above every name, so that at the name of Jesus every knee should bend, in heaven and on earth and under the earth, and every tongue should confess that Jesus Christ is Lord, to the glory of God the Father.

Philippians 2:5–11

In today's world of hubris, egotism, and self-promotion, humility is often undervalued and misunderstood. It is not self-abasement and false modesty, where we deny our abilities and successes. Rather, it is our realistic appraisal of both our strengths and our weaknesses. Without humility, we cannot continue to learn and grow. It is very close kin to unselfishness, for we are unlikely to be more concerned for others' needs than our own if we have too much pride—if we think we are better, more important, or more fortunate than others.[1]

I confess: humility is not my strong suit. I was proud of my independence, of my ability to do whatever I needed to do to accomplish the tasks before me. Years ago, a friend who was a family counselor observed, "Ella, you habitually bite off more than you can chew . . . and then proceed to chew it." I thought of it as "carving up the elephant": dividing huge, complex projects into manageable pieces. I enjoyed the challenge, and stress was my ally—pushing me to stay focused and on task.

As a widow, my self-reliance, my determination to be independent, and my efforts to prove that I could manage Lev's affairs were driven as much by my pride as by my desire not to be a burden on my children.

Eventually, I acknowledged that no matter how hard I worked and studied, I could not learn all that Lev knew from decades of managing our family affairs. I did not understand finance and investments as well as my bankers did; legal documents as well as my attorney did; or income, expenses, and taxes as well as my accountant did. I did not grasp the complexities of insurance. However, if I lay aside my false pride and admitted my inadequacies, I could ask questions and learn from my advisors. The learning curve was steep, and it took me a painfully long time to become comfortable with unfamiliar financial and legal terms and concepts. Though I never read a contract before Lev died, now I waded through legalese in order to have a basic understanding of all that I was being asked to sign.

I discovered that I simply could not do some things well. That was painful for me to accept, because for sixty-eight years I operated in arenas where my best was good enough. Now it was not. I am not a numbers person. I had to have help—more help than Lev ever needed. I dared not keep the books for the business, but I did not abdicate my responsibility. I reviewed every bill and every bank statement. I signed every check.

Simple tasks discouraged me, too. I needed the yardman to change light bulbs and retrieve items from high shelves. I pressed repairmen to perform extra chores when they were at the house. I had to humble myself and accept the reality that I required more people to take care of me alone than we had needed as a couple. I had to give myself permission to do things differently than Lev had, paying for many of the tasks that he had performed so effortlessly through the years. Yes, our friend Ralph was right when he said that Lev had made my life very easy.

Father Jonathan Morris described me in his *New York Times* bestseller, *The Way to Serenity*:

> If we examine discouragement closely, we find some things that may surprise us. The first is that discouragement stems not from an excess of humility but from an excess of pride. We often have such a high opinion of ourselves that when we don't perform to the standards we set for ourselves we become disheartened. We exaggerate our own importance, as if our weakness and sins were somehow weightier than God's mercy and goodness.
>
> Sometimes, too, discouragement emerges because we don't know ourselves very well. We have an inflated idea of ourselves and of our own virtue, so when we fail we feel surprised, confused, and ashamed and we want to give up. But here the pain comes not so much from having failed and offended God but from wounded self-love. We are embarrassed and humiliated at seeing ourselves so weak.[2]

Throughout my married life, I sometimes traveled alone and thought nothing of dining alone. Even at home, I often took a break from errands to eat a quick lunch by myself. Despite that, Lev and I were together virtually every evening, weekend, and holiday; and I pitied those who were alone. For Lev, *home* was critically important because he had little experience with *home* growing up. He was only eight when he was sent away to boarding school. As an adult, he did not enjoy "guy" trips or sports. He did not fish, hunt, or play golf. He rarely traveled on business. When he was not working, he wanted to be home with his family.

Suddenly, as a widow, empty hours—like empty chairs—contributed to the black hole in which I found myself. As I searched for role models among the widows whom I knew, I also observed the widows whom I did not want to emulate, the ones I had pitied when I was half a couple. I did not want anyone to feel sorry for me because I was alone. I quit eating by myself in restaurants where friends might see me and insist that I join their table. Instead, I went to out-of-the-way places where I was unlikely to be recognized. One of the appeals of Dallas was that I was anonymous. I could go by myself to the symphony, opera, or a neighborhood restaurant and no one pitied me. No one felt an obligation to reach out to me.

While every widow has her own list of sinkholes—those occasions when her aloneness overwhelms her—some are common to most widows I know.

Attending church services was surprisingly hard. I felt alone in a sea of couples. I expected my church to be a major source of comfort and companionship, but it was not. People were friendly and compassionate, but I missed having Lev beside me in the pew. Sunday lunch was perhaps when I felt most conspicuously alone.

Going to a big luncheon or dinner alone was intimidating: walking up to a table with two empty chairs—the other six or eight occupied by couples—and asking if I could join them, suffering the humiliation of being turned away because they were saving places for another couple, or sitting down and having a couple come in later who could not find two places together. Assigned tables and place cards were a welcome relief... except when all the single women were relegated to the same table.

Grandchildren's weddings and other major family events were agonizing. *Lev is supposed to be here!* As the oldest grandson's big church wedding approached in 2012, I panicked at the thought of being escorted down the aisle and sitting by myself on the second row. After I finally confessed my anxiety, the bride's mother resolved my crisis by seating the grandparents on the first row with the parents of the bride and groom.

Holidays were worst of all. Even the remote possibility that I might be alone on a day when everyone in the world seemed to be with family caused major anxiety that set in weeks, even months in advance and was alleviated only when Peggy's and

Lev's plans were finalized and I knew where I would be. I had never spent Christmas Eve or Christmas night by myself. When I was half a couple, Lev and I could leave Peggy and Scott's ranch at noon on Christmas Day and drive home to spend a quiet evening together in front of the fire or the tree . . . or we could take an afternoon flight to Colorado Springs and stay at the Broadmoor, enjoying the mountains and snow and lavish decorations. As a new widow, even the thought of coming home alone to an empty house after spending the day with my family terrified me. My stress was contagious, affecting Peggy most of all, since I depended on her to coordinate all the family plans.

Just as I was proud of my competence and my marital status, I was proud to have caring, dependable children and counted myself blessed to have a daughter living in the same community. I did not want to ask for help from friends. While I was generally not afraid of being in the house alone, the possibility of being sick or injured and alone frightened me. Except for college, I had never lived away from family. When I was ill, I called Peggy. When I was in a car accident, I called Peggy. When my car died late at night, I called Peggy. When I had knee surgery, I depended on Peggy. I never had to call a neighbor in the middle of the night. I never had to ask a friend to provide transportation or go to the grocery store for me. More than five years after Lev died, I finally began to lay aside my pride to ask for and accept help graciously.

Rarely overwhelmed by worries or depression, I also prided myself on my emotional strength and self-control. I kept my composure and displayed strength in the immediate aftermath of Lev's death, only to be beset by fear and anxiety later.

Fortunately, I had a caring physician who recognized my need for emotional help. During my annual physical, I described my stress and anxiety attacks. She gently inquired about my responsibilities, then said, "You need to be fully functioning. I'm going to prescribe an anti-depressant/anti-anxiety medication that will take the edge off without making you a zombie. You probably won't even feel the effect, but your family will notice the difference, and they will thank me."

She very carefully supervised my drug use, starting slowly and very gradually increasing the dosage. This was a medication to take daily, not on an as-needed basis. It worked. The anxiety subsided. I slept better. I could swallow. I never graduated to a full dose. By Thanksgiving, I thought I could do without it (we all want to be strong), but the stress was too great leading up to Christmas. After the first of the year, I began reducing the dosage again, and this time I had no problems. I was drug-free within a few weeks.

When I returned to my doctor a year later, I reported that I was generally doing well but that I still had occasional panic attacks where I badly overreacted, times when I could not "turn off my mind" from worry to sleep at night. This time she gave me a different anti-anxiety drug to take as needed. I never took more than half a tablet a day, and a prescription of fifteen tended to last about six months. I learned to recognize the symptoms early—a tight chest or rapidly beating heart.

I wish I were "strong" enough or—more accurately—mellow enough never to need a psychotropic drug, but I am thankful for a wise doctor who enabled me to function and for family who cut me slack when I overreacted. In the beginning, I thought that if I worked very hard, I would finish all the tasks that had to be done. In what I came to think of as The Depression of Year 2, I realized that the "job" is never done. Widowhood is a journey, not a destination. I have new responsibilities. I continue to change in unpredictable, not-always-healthy ways. I continually need to humble myself and ask for help.

❁

Lesson learned: When we let go of our false pride and acknowledge the areas where we need help from others, we cultivate an attitude and an atmosphere where we can learn and grow.

11

Serenity

Therefore, my beloved, just as you have always obeyed me, not only in my presence, but much more now in my absence, work out your own salvation with fear and trembling; for it is God who is at work in you, enabling you both to will and to work for his good pleasure. Do all things without murmuring and arguing, so that you may be blameless and innocent, children of God without blemish in the midst of a crooked and perverse generation, in which you shine like stars in the world. It is by your holding fast to the word of life that I can boast on the day of Christ that I did not run in vain or labor in vain.

Philippians 2:12–16

In most situations, I did not lack courage, but I struggled to find serenity and wisdom. I lay awake nights weighing options and possibilities, searching for ways to be a force for positive change. Meek acceptance of circumstances was not my nature.

Mama was a worrier, and I grew up hearing Daddy lecture her. *Worrying is pointless. If you can do something about it, do it. If you can't, let it go.* I preferred his attitude to hers, and somewhere I acquired the naïve confidence to believe that I could be whomever I chose to be, that I could change almost anything if I wanted to badly enough.

My problem as a new widow was figuring out what I could change. I found it easy to ruminate about a past I could not change and to worry about a future I could not know. I could not always let go immediately; but to a great degree, I could keep my mind from getting stuck on thoughts that made me sad and anxious. While I could not change my circumstances, I could change my reaction to them. I loved the quotation attributed to Martin Luther: *we can't keep the birds from flying over our heads, but we can keep them from nesting in our hair.*

Seeking peace, I continually prayed the Serenity Prayer, another gift from my friend Betty, who also taught me how to live in gratitude mode.

> God grant me the serenity to accept the things I cannot change,
> Courage to change the things I can,
> And wisdom to know the difference.[1]

To achieve serenity, I had to accept and acknowledge my limitations and embrace my new role. I did not like my new status—*widow*—neither the circumstances that made me a widow nor the images the word conjured up. I neither liked the fine print in Lev's will and trust nor the impact those terms had on my life. I did not like what felt like an invasion of my privacy, that all these people had to know all my financial affairs.

This person with whom I had shared my feelings openly for forty-six years was gone, and I had no one to take his place. To whom else could I complain at the end of a bad day, fret about the children and grandchildren, worry about finances . . . or dream about the future?

For the longest time, I tried to delude everyone, including myself. I wore a mask of strength and stoic acceptance, not admitting my pain and loneliness to anyone—not even Lev IV and Peggy. I wanted to be steady and undemonstrative like Daddy, not emotional like Mama. But in times of stress and pressure, my buried feelings bubbled to the surface and spilled out in harmful ways. I grumbled. I complained. I overreacted and spoke harsh, angry words. I certainly was not blameless in the tension that mounted within the family in the months after Lev's death.

Reflecting on Year 1 of widowhood, I am grateful for those who helped me move from anger, fear, and anxiety to acceptance and serenity.

Paul, our former minister who filled the role of family priest, dropped his responsibilities and cancelled his appointments as a college president living hundreds of miles away to come to us when he received word of Lev's death. He completely lifted the burden of planning the memorial service from us. For more than a year afterwards, he called "just to chat" on the seventh of every month.

Sol, Lev's accountant for more than thirty years, devoted most of his working hours to helping me, filling the void when Lev's financial advisors resigned. He had the history and memory that we needed. When nothing was in writing to give me direction, I could count on Sol to remember how Lev had handled it or would want it handled. He continually encouraged me, "You can do it."

After Lev's service, friends gave me hugs and promised that they would be back in touch after I had time to rest and recover. They did not know how desperately I needed people around me to fill the void left by Lev's departure. I did not know what I was supposed to do in the evening. I did not know how to play this role. In summary, I did not know how to go on living as a single.

I looked for a mentor; and I remembered Alice, a reed-slim, elegant blonde, widowed for more than twenty years. Her life was full, meaningful, and well balanced. She held significant leadership roles in her community and her church, she was involved in her children's and grandchildren's lives, and she was committed to her friends. If she could create a good new life for herself, so could I. We had known each other for more than forty years. Our daughters had gone to school together and were good friends. I called her to ask, "Please go to dinner with me and tell me what I am supposed to do." Her advice was the best I received and is what I pass on to new widows now.

They will not give you time to grieve. You cannot do it alone. You need to get someone to help you.

Lev IV and Peggy were continually available to me throughout the long process of settling the estate. They were trustworthy and loyal, even when we disagreed and even when I overreacted. I was fortunate to have this kind of support. Not every widow does.

Eventually, with a lot of help and prayer, I made it over, under, and around the boulders that blocked my way as I climbed up that unfamiliar mountain. I did not keep a journal of the craziness and haziness of that first year. I wanted to look forward, not dwell on the past. However, I have often wished that I had kept a list of the many things that I had to do for the first time. That list would be long and would range from the trivial to learning and managing Lev's business; reading contracts; and hiring new bankers, lawyers, and insurance agents.

Virtually every new task reminded me of Lev's absence. I was the spoiled wife of a good, successful man—poorly prepared for new responsibilities. All those "firsts" were not only difficult but also depressing reminders that I was alone now. Other widows agreed that those things we did when we were married were easier to do later, as widows.

Models of serenity were not hard to find. I thought of my trips to the heartland of Buddhism: Sri Lanka, Thailand, Cambodia, and Laos. I thought all the women were beautiful, gentle, and graceful; and I felt clumsy, awkward, and loud in comparison. A hard-driving, tightly wound, French-born New York businessman who boasted of his atheism and materialism was so impressed by our guide's serenity in Chiang Mai that he began meeting with her privately to understand Buddhism better. In Sri Lanka, where I spent two weeks on a construction mission team after the 2004 tsunami, the people's serenity as they faced the future without loved ones, without homes, and without other possessions awed me. But most bewildering and awe-inspiring of all were our guides in Cambodia, as they led us through the killing fields and prisons of the Pol Pot regime. They described being taken from their families as young children to live naked in the forests as slave laborers. As I learned the horrific consequences of American carpet bombing during the Vietnam War and our veto of humanitarian aid afterwards, I marveled that these people could welcome us to their country.

I saw the same serenity in the faces of elderly saints of the church: nuns in their habits, their faces radiant, reflecting their inner peace, serenity, and goodness.

Closer to home, I saw this same inner beauty in some of the saints of First Baptist Church, and I asked two of them— Beverly and her good friend Mary Ann T—to serve as my spiritual mentors. We met for lunch several times a year, where they shared their walks through widowhood and their serene acceptance of living in the winter of their lives. They answered my questions, prayed for me, and read some of my manuscript. I had known both women for almost fifty years through Baylor alumni and church activities, though I originally met Mary Ann in a backyard art fair when she sold her very first painting.

While Beverly's leadership ability was obvious to me from the beginning, I viewed Mary Ann more as a quiet, supportive wife and mother. I served with her husband, Louis, a geologist, and taught their children in high school Sunday School, while Mary Ann taught my children and countless others in the church nursery. I underestimated this pretty, always smiling, always friendly, hospitable, soft-spoken woman. She surprised me when Louis died. She learned to pump her own gas and to manage Louis' business interests. She volunteered to share teaching responsibilities with Beverly in the oldest women's Sunday School class. For many years, Beverly, Mary Ann, and their husbands had led senior adult trips around the world. As widows, Beverly and Mary Ann continued to travel together. Though a stroke slowed Mary Ann down a little, she still went to the gym daily, still gardened, still painted, still saw her friends regularly, and still traveled often.

Not every widow was like me, denying the possibility of widowhood, refusing to learn all that I needed to know about my husband's responsibilities. My childhood friend Betty Ann wrote me:

> Bob had prostate surgery in 1992. It had spread; and the doctor told me he would probably live four to five years, even with radiation. I never told Bob that! We found out on September 10, 2001, that it was back; and we knew there were no more treatments. Once we were over the initial shock, we started making some sort of plan. He really wasn't feeling too bad then. He was still working, and I was teaching. We decided I needed to learn how to do some things around the house. Bob was the original Mr. Fix-it, so we had very few repair people out during the thirty-seven years we were married.
>
> I got a notebook, and we started. First, I listed where everything was on the computer and in the files. Then Bob taught me how to change out sockets, make small repairs, drain the water heater; and we stocked a tool kit for me. He showed me how the TVs were connected. He did all the wiring. I had about six pages full of notes. I wish I still had them.
>
> You know, when you know it is coming, you react differently. Everything we did, we did with gusto. We even enjoyed our trips to the grocery store; and when he would tire, he loved those motorized carts. I have wonderful memories of those months and lots of good stories for the kids . . . like what to do with his ashes. Bob accepted his death with dignity. He said there would be no mully-grubbing and he meant it. I was blessed!

Betty Ann had five months to learn how to manage her life before Bob entered hospice. Though Lev and I had not taken the precautionary steps they took, Sol was correct. I reached the top of the mountain. I reached it when I could remember the early months of widowhood without reliving them, when I could abandon my false pride and admit my pain and my fears.

I reached the top when I quit trying to escape the reality of my aloneness and welcomed solitude, where I could spend time in reflection. In finally allowing myself to admit and then process my grief, I sorted out what I could change and what I could not. With new wisdom, I achieved a degree of serenity and peace.

Yes, I finally reached the top of the mountain, but then I discovered that the journey does not end there. I continue to fall into unexpected sinkholes from time to time. However, when I look back, I can see how far I have come. Those halting steps up the mountain added up. Life is good. I am content. Increasingly, my spirit soars and I experience real joy.

❉

Lesson learned: Before we can find serenity, we must process our grief and acknowledge that we are helpless to change our circumstances. When we accept the reality of our loss and all that it means, we can claim the wisdom and serenity that lead to joy.

12

Again, Joy

But even if I am being poured out as a libation over the sacrifice and the offering of your faith, I am glad and rejoice with all of you—and in the same way you also must be glad and rejoice with me.

Philippians 2:17, 18

It's called "the ministry of presence"—simply being there with someone who is sick, dying, hurting, or grieving. No words are necessary. Presence is not only a ministry; it is a gift, one that I desperately needed.

Though I sometimes felt alone in the crowd, smiling bravely to hide my pain, I still preferred being with family or friends—with anyone, in fact—to being alone. During the day I was busy; but when half past five came, the time Lev always walked in the back door from the office, I panicked. What was I supposed to do for the next five hours?

I took pride in doing what had to be done to settle the estate. I gradually gained confidence in myself as I learned to work with my professional advisors and mastered the basics of Lev's business. I began to think that God had heard my prayers for wisdom and discernment.

Reclaiming joy took far longer. For at least four years after Lev's death, I ran away from emptiness, loneliness, and silence. Though "Lev work" demanded my full attention in Year 1, I was unwilling to relinquish the activities that had given me purpose and fulfillment throughout the years of our marriage, so I packed every minute of every day with busyness.

During the years of Lev's declining health, I dropped out of much of the club and nonprofit work that had consumed me for most of my adult life. Afterwards, thanks to well-meaning friends who thought that I needed something to do with what they assumed was all my free time, I added hours of work when I joined six nonprofit boards scattered across Texas.

About the same time, I undertook a couple of big, personally satisfying, "Ella work" projects—redecorating and renovating my Corpus Christi home and garden; and buying, remodeling, and furnishing a condo in Dallas, where Lev IV and his family lived. I adored my grandsons, and they adored me, but they were young adults. I recognized that if I wanted to be part of their lives, I needed to go to them.

And I began to travel again.

Anxious about Lev's approaching birthday, I decided that I wanted to return to New Orleans, my birthplace, where Lev and I had spent so many long weekends. Early in our marriage, I introduced Lev to that city, and he embraced it fully—from jazz to Cajun food. Our home was full of antiques bought in New Orleans. It was a place full of joyous memories.

Many of those memories included our longtime friends and neighbors, Jo and Richard, with whom we shared and celebrated March birthdays. We met them shortly after Richard opened his orthodontics practice in 1974. Through the years, our lives intersected in our church, clubs, neighborhood, and our girls—from summer camp to college sorority. Jo and I considered each other the sister we never had. I asked them to go with me. We prowled the French Quarter, enjoyed Creole and Cajun cooking at old favorites and new finds, walked the streets of the Garden District, and rode the streetcar out St. Charles Avenue. The trip was a pilgrimage that brought closure.

In my travels I tried a little of everything: two grand trips to Asia with luxury tour companies, cruises, and travel in the United States and abroad with various nonprofit organizations. Sometimes the group was what mattered, but often no one I knew was interested in a particular event or destination on my bucket list. I chose to travel with strangers rather than stay home. Unlike many of my friends, I sometimes traveled without Lev during our marriage, so I was not terribly intimidated by traveling solo now. Still, I started slowly.

I spent a few days alone in Paris before taking the train to Maastricht in The Netherlands, where I joined friends at The European Fine Arts Fair.

I sandwiched a week in Carmel with friends between a few days alone in San Francisco and Los Angeles.

Then, in September 2011, I took a giant step when I flew to London for a few days before taking the train to Edinburgh, where I joined a group of strangers from the Colonial Williamsburg Foundation for a rail tour of Scotland. That was the first of many trips with an outstanding group of like-minded travel companions. On every trip with the group, I joined old friends and made new ones, building a network of acquaintances across the country and finding community in Williamsburg.

As a widow, I found that travel with nonprofit affinity groups such as Colonial Williamsburg met my needs best. Fellow travelers were more welcoming than those on cruise ships and luxury commercial operations. I no longer feared joining a group of strangers, for I knew we shared common interests and they would not stay strangers long. Demographics mattered, and I looked at the average age and marital status of the travelers, the size of the group, how many meals were included in the package, and whether alcoholic beverages were included. Couples were more likely to invite me to join them if they knew that they would not get stuck with my bar tab.

By trial and error, I learned that I was more comfortable returning alone to places where I was awash in good memories of previous visits with Lev than exploring unfamiliar places. With the exception of London, which Lev and I always considered "halfway home," charming villages held more appeal than high-energy big cities. Alone in places where I could safely walk quaint streets filled with beauty and history, my stress and anxiety evaporated. I was not lonely in my aloneness.

I learned never to assume that someone would be available to assist me with my luggage, so I purchased smaller, lightweight, four-wheeled luggage and carried only what I could personally handle and lift. Other travelers stopped and stared at airports when I effortlessly removed my checked suitcases from the conveyor belt, raised the handles, attached my carry-on bag and my purse on top, and casually walked off with stacked bags on each side.

Aesthetics mattered: I desired a serene room with a good view—mountains, water, forests, or flowers. I preferred small hotels in safe locations, with knowledgeable concierges and good restaurants close by. Since travel for one is never as expensive as travel for two, I allowed myself to spend more to ensure my safety and well-being as a single, older woman. After several unpleasant experiences with cab drivers, I began to ask my hotel to arrange for a car to take me to and from the airport. I learned to use the Uber app on my cell phone, eliminating the need to stand on the curb to flag down a passing cab.

One sinkhole repeatedly tripped me up. When I traveled alone as a wife, I left the house in Lev's capable hands and I returned home to his embrace. I called almost every evening to describe my day. As a new widow, I suffered from surprising anxiety attacks each time I secured and then left the house for a trip. I had no one to talk to at night when I traveled; and I returned to a dark, empty, unwelcoming house. With time, I adjusted to living alone and my anxiety subsided, though it has never completely disappeared.

By 2013 I had to acknowledge that parts of my life were not satisfying or fulfilling. I concluded that this was not a temporary situation caused by grief but an indication of changes occurring in my psyche.

I still loved our home, but it did not function for me alone as it had for us as a couple. In another round of redecorating, I lightened and brightened the walls, replaced heavy bedspreads with lightweight bed coverings, and added flat-screen televisions in the bedrooms. I removed the hot tub and turned a porch into an outdoor room.

Lev always planned to retain active management of his business interests and keep his downtown office until he died. There, too, I gave myself permission to do it differently. When I finally turned over the last account to professional managers, I felt like I had retired.

In retirement, I did not want my calendar filled with meetings I felt obligated to attend. After fifty years, I found nonprofit board work depleting rather than fulfilling. I took my fiduciary responsibilities as a director seriously, and I was increasingly frustrated by boards with an "if it ain't broke, don't fix it" attitude. At the same time, I no longer wanted the stress that came with board debate. I was ready for younger people to take charge.

Wanting to change my lifestyle and facing the heat of Texas summer, I recalled a cold visit to Maine in June 1986, when Lev and I drove from Portland to Bar Harbor. We dreamed of returning to those quaint fishing villages and artists' communities. I signed up for a Maine coastal cruise with a group from the Smithsonian Institution, flying to Boston for a few days before joining the group in Portland. Afterwards, I went to Nantucket, which Lev and I had visited on a day trip by ferry from Cape Cod years earlier.

I originally planned to spend a week on Nantucket, but I was afraid to be completely alone for so long on that remote island thirty miles out in the Atlantic. I decided that four days would be bearable. Four years and four months after Lev died, as I walked the cobblestone streets of Nantucket, I finally found joy that lasted more than a moment. I discovered a serene, tranquil beauty and peace that caused my spirit to soar and led me to reevaluate and ultimately repurpose my life. For the very first time, I thought that perhaps I should write a book—a handbook for new widows. I knew that writing required solitude, and I did not know if I was ready to spend time alone with my memories. I returned a year later to see whether my peace and joy were real or whether I had imagined it all.

In the interim, I had two flashes of exuberant joy beyond the simple pleasures of time with family and close friends, feasting on great music, or losing myself in a great book.

I arrived in Sydney, Australia, on Australia Day 2014, after a long cruise through rough waters. After checking into my hotel on a hill overlooking the harbor, I opened the curtains in my room and saw the biggest party that I had ever witnessed. Every kind of floating vessel was in the harbor. People were hiking over the top of the iconic bridge across the water. Parachutists holding Australian flags jumped from planes. South of the harbor, young people celebrated with food, music, and booze in the historic Rocks district. The walkways to the opera house were packed. In uncharacteristic fashion, I wanted to be part of it; so I plunged into the crowds that jammed Sydney. That evening I walked alone, again through throngs of merrymakers, to a sidewalk café, where I joined the crowd watching the fireworks. It was my most exhilarating day in recent memory. Never once did I feel unsafe, uneasy, or lonely. I was simply thrilled by every moment of the celebration.

Several months later, I joined a Colonial Williamsburg group for a tour of historic Philadelphia with interpreters/impersonators of Thomas Jefferson and James Madison. After dinner in a grand historic building in an old part of the city, which Mr. Jefferson and Mr. Madison attended in eighteenth-century formal attire, we passed a seedy bar where a prostitute loitered outside. I suggested to my seatmate on the bus that we should take Madison and Jefferson to the bar and watch the reaction. Somehow, that incongruous image set her off in a peal of contagious laughter. Soon, I was laughing as hard as she was. We so surprised our fellow travelers that they jokingly accused us of disturbing their peace and drinking too much. Alone back in my hotel room, I reflected on my laughter and my friends' reaction. I realized that they first met me on the train trip across Scotland seventeen months after Lev died. They never knew me as Lev's wife. They probably had never heard me laugh aloud before, because it was the first time I had enjoyed such unrestrained laughter since his death.

My unrestrained joy in Nantucket on my return trip a few months later was a different kind of joy that flowed from the peace I found there. I was able to cast aside all my worries and fears and live in the present, finding happiness in the days I was alone as surely as in the days when I was joined by family and friends. Each summer I stayed longer. By 2016, it was my summer home.

❊

Lesson learned: We are more likely to know ourselves, to search our hearts, and to reflect on our emotional reactions and their meaning in solitude than in crowds. When we develop self-understanding, we take a giant step toward experiencing joy.

13

Friendship

I hope in the Lord Jesus to send Timothy to you soon, so that I may be cheered by news of you. I have no one like him who will be genuinely concerned for your welfare. All of them are seeking their own interests, not those of Jesus Christ. But Timothy's worth you know, how like a son with a father he has served with me in the work of the gospel. I hope therefore to send him as soon as I see how things go with me; and I trust in the Lord that I will also come soon.

Philippians 2:19–24

My mother-in-law, Helen, always had an innate sense of the value of friendship, of how to be a friend. She was a small-town girl from East Texas who married into wealth and privilege. During the course of her first marriage, she moved from Tyler to Tulsa to Oklahoma City to San Antonio and on to Miami and Orlando during World War II, then back to Oklahoma City before relocating to San Antonio in 1948. In all those moves she made friends, and she maintained those friendships despite distance and three marriages. Whether she was on the telephone, writing notes, or entertaining, she made her friends a priority. She was generous and thoughtful, there for them in bad times as well as good times.

I grew up in very different circumstances in Texarkana. Mama had her friends from church, while Daddy, a railroad man, had his fishing buddies from work. They did not have couple friends, and they rarely entertained. Growing up in that loving but quiet, unsocial household, I was an introvert—studious and religious—with minimal social skills and few close friends. In college I found friends at the student newspaper and the honors program. As a bride in a strange city, I had no idea how to make friends or entertain.

Helen, my mentor in so many areas, advised me to join every group I could. She was right when she said, "In almost every group, you will find two or three people who will become lasting friends."

Looking back decades later, I can still name the organizations and events where I met my oldest, closest friends. Many of my friendships date back to an invitation for beer and tamales in Phyllis and Sam's back yard on Labor Day 1964. Lev knew them before they married, and I met Phyllis when she returned to the *Caller-Times*, where she had worked before her marriage, in summer 1962 to fill in for another reporter on vacation. She and Sam, a Realtor, both grew up in Corpus Christi, and they seemed to know everybody. Though they hardly knew me, they invited us to their party. They filled their back yard with a crowd that included many couples who, like us, were newcomers. Their parties continued for fifty years, with annual holiday traditions.

Helen's words proved true again when Lev died. As I joined new boards and spent increasing time in Dallas, Waco, Williamsburg, and Nantucket, I met women with similar interests and values. While I strengthened my bonds with my friends at home, I also formed new friendships across the country.

Her advice never to say "no" to a social invitation if I could say "yes" also served me well. Friends soon learned that if I was already cooking my dinner when they called, I would put the half-cooked meal in the refrigerator or the garbage can and go out.

Mama Wall, my grandmother, was an unlikely role model whose attitude toward life confirmed Helen's advice. She was a very large woman with serious circulation problems—just getting in and out of the car was an ordeal. When she was almost one hundred, she made the long drive from northeast Louisiana to Corpus Christi to visit. I marveled at her willingness to make the trip. She explained, "I hurt whether I'm alone in my room or out. Going out isn't going to make it any worse, and when I'm out I enjoy myself and forget my aches and pains." Similarly, I tended to forget my aching loneliness when I went out with friends.

Loneliness is a killer. Literally. Dr. Dhruv Khullar calls social isolation "a growing epidemic—one that's increasingly recognized as having dire physical, mental and emotional consequences. . . . Human connection lies at the heart of human well-being."

Regrettably, new widows often withdraw from their friends, increasing their grief, anxiety, and depression. Dr. Khullar cites the evidence:

> Individuals with less social connection have disrupted sleep patterns, altered immune systems, more inflammation and higher levels of stress hormones. One recent study found that isolation increases the risk of heart disease by 29 percent and stroke by 32 percent. . . .
>
> Loneliness can accelerate cognitive decline in older adults, and isolated individuals are twice as likely to die prematurely as those with more robust social interactions. . . . All told, loneliness is as important a risk factor for early death as obesity and smoking.[1]

For those women who were caregivers, social isolation is a serious issue. Often, they withdraw from social interactions to care for their husbands. Reconnecting can be a challenge.

While I was never a full-time caregiver and Lev went to his office daily until four months before his death, our world had narrowed. Because he tired easily and fell often, we quit attending large parties. While we occasionally went to dinner with old friends, I no longer entertained at home. I was not a "lady who lunched" or played cards. Ours had been a social world of couples, and my friends were almost exclusively the wives of his friends. When Lev died, they were there for me—bringing food, serving meals, supporting me at his service.

Blogger John Pavlovitz described it best.

> When you lose someone you love—people show up.
>
> Almost immediately they surround you with social media condolences and texts and visits and meals and flowers. They come with good hearts, with genuine compassion, and they truly want to support you in those moments. . . .
>
> The early days of grief are a hazy, dizzying, moment by moment response to a trauma that your mind simply can't wrap itself around. You are, what I like to call a *Grief Zombie;* outwardly moving but barely there. You aren't really functioning normally by any reasonable measurement, and so that huge crush of people is like diverting thousands of cars into a one lane back road—it all overwhelms the system. You can't absorb it all. Often it actually hurts.
>
> This usually happens until the day of the funeral, when almost immediately the flood of support begins to subside. Over the coming days the calls and visits gradually become less frequent as people begin to return to their normal lives already in progress—right about the time the bottom drops out for you.
>
> Just as the shock begins to wear off and the haze is lifted and you start to feel the full gravity of the loss; just as you get a clear look at the massive crater in your heart—you find yourself alone.
>
> People don't leave you because they're callous or unconcerned, they're just unaware. Most people understand grief as an *event,* not as the permanent alteration to life that it is, and so they stay up until the funeral and imagine that when the service ends, that somehow you too can move ahead; that there is some *finishing* to your mourning.[2]

I encountered much the same, and other widows report similar experiences. All but your closest friends withdraw. Invitations to dinner dry up. But while those were unexpected losses on top of losing Lev, I realized unexpected gains as well. Single acquaintances—divorced, widowed, never married—surprised me by their outpouring of love and concern. That sisterhood proved invaluable, for they understood what I was going through. I could be honest with them about my pain and fear because they had been there. They had reached the point of acceptance. Their example gave me hope.

I felt unworthy of their friendship because I had been one of those thoughtless women who was not a good friend to my widowed and divorced friends. I had not realized how alone they were. Now I tried to atone. To those not-always-single women who reached out to me, who called me to go to dinner or the movies or Las Vegas, I said, "I do not deserve this. I was not a good friend. I did not realize . . ."

My parents reared me to live by the Golden Rule: *Do to others as you would have them do to you* (Luke 6:31). That came naturally in most aspects of my life, but somehow, I had never visualized myself as single. I had no idea what I would want and need in this role, and so I had no empathy for friends who reached this place ahead of me.

Five women in particular made a significant difference in my life.

Renee was my first friend in Corpus Christi. She was quick to reach out to me when we met in the Art Museum Auxiliary shortly after I married, and she and her husband drew Lev and me into their circle of friends and their clubs. We remained friends through her divorce and remarriage; but tragically, Henry, her second husband, died of lymphoma within a few years. Like most young widows, Renee went back to work; and we drifted apart. A reading specialist, Renee stayed active and engaged, tutoring young children four days a week. She was a regular at the gym, trim and fit and energetic.

LaRae, a retired teacher, divorced for twenty years, lived just a few blocks from me. We had briefly worked together in the Junior League in the 1970s, our daughters were the same age, and we had many mutual friends. But we seldom saw each other socially. Our paths simply did not cross. How surprised I was when she called and invited me to go to dinner with her. She became one of my most dependable friends, always ready for a meal or a trip. Upbeat and positive, she was always fun to be with.

Like Renee and LaRae, so many stay-at-home wives find themselves suddenly single long before they are eligible for Medicare and Social Security. With young adult children and few peers, they need health insurance and a reason to get up in the morning. They are forced to drop out of daytime women's groups, and they find themselves excluded from most couples' social activities in the evening and on the weekend. After retirement they are eager to reestablish their social lives.

Mary Anne's situation was somewhat different. As a fashion designer and later a residential real estate agent, her hours were flexible. A glamorous brunette with a dramatic flair, she founded Clowns Who Care, a group of women who entertained at the local children's hospital. She had a huge network of friends—all ages, single and married. I was dimly aware of Mary Anne throughout my married life. After she and Bob married, we saw them periodically at parties but never knew them well. When Bob died of cancer in 1999, I never thought to reach out to her. But she reached out to me after Lev died; and we discovered we had a lot in common, from history to art to fashion to mutual friends. She, like me, always preferred eating out to eating at home alone.

Kathy and Bub were among those Lev and I met in Phyllis and Sam's backyard. Kathy and Lev recognized each other; they had been neighbors in San Antonio as little children. Soon they and their three-year-old were like family to us. When they came to dinner at our house, we piled phone books in a chair so that their little daughter could sit at the table with us. When Bub was stricken with cancer in 2001, I stayed away because I did not know what to say. While we continued to see Kathy occasionally, I was never there for her in the way she was for me after Lev died. A tall, slender brunette, always impeccably groomed, Kathy stayed active in her church, clubs, and volunteer work as a widow.

I had known Louise and John for fifty years. We were members of some of the same clubs, and John's younger sister was a friend. Louise, a geologist, moved to Corpus Christi to work for Humble Oil Company (now Exxon) in the fifties. Shortly afterwards, John, a very successful farmer, and Louise met in a Sunday School class for young singles, and their romance flourished. With no children, they were each other's best friends; and together they provided strong leadership for the city's civic, cultural, and social institutions. After several years of declining health, John died one year before Lev. She was still grieving deeply in 2009 when our lives intersected again.

Others reached out as well; but these women all lived near me, making it easy to get together in the evening. Since each of them had more experience as a single than I, they taught me how to enjoy life without Lev and how to be a friend. They introduced me to their friends and included me in their activities. We discovered mutual friends, and new friend groups formed. I learned much more about art and classical music, I went to lots more movies, and I tried more new restaurants because of their friendship. I have tried to pay it forward by befriending those who arrived at this place after me.

❋

Lesson learned: True friends genuinely care for us and want the best for us. They are there for us in the bad times as well as the good times.

14

Hospitality

Still, I think it necessary to send to you Epaphroditus—my brother and co-worker and fellow soldier, your messenger and minister to my need; for he has been longing for all of you, and has been distressed because you heard that he was ill. He was indeed so ill that he nearly died. But God had mercy on him, and not only on him but on me also, so that I would not have one sorrow after another. I am the more eager to send him, therefore, in order that you may rejoice at seeing him again, and that I may be less anxious. Welcome him then in the Lord with all joy, and honor such people, because he came close to death for the work of Christ, risking his life to make up for those services that you could not give me.

Philippians 2:25–30

A native son was returning home to Philippi; and the Apostle Paul, writing from his prison cell in Rome, instructed this small, struggling congregation to welcome Epaphroditus with joy. From beginning to end, the Bible is full of injunctions to be welcoming and hospitable. I tend to think of hospitality as a gift, and we all know people who excel in entertaining, who have a knack for making everyone feel comfortable and welcome. However, Paul—who had a lot to say about spiritual gifts—did not include hospitality on his lists of gifts that some might possess. Instead, he wrote unequivocally to the Romans, *Practice hospitality* (Rom 12:13b, NIV). Widows are not exempt. Instead of throwing pity parties for ourselves, we can fill our homes with friends.

For whatever reason, we widows seem to forget how to entertain. We slip into neutral gear, waiting for others to invite us. But never have friends been so important. In place of that companion who was always there, we need a multitude of relationships to fill the void.

Extraverts like Phyllis draw their energy from people, so they instinctively gather others around them. I am shyer, more introverted—more comfortable planning a big party and mailing formal invitations than calling a casual acquaintance to meet me for dinner. Deep down, I fear rejection. But the worst thing that can happen is that someone will say "no."

When Lev was alive, I preferred reacting to others' invitations rather than initiating get-togethers myself. I was content spending evenings with him. But after Lev's death, I quickly realized that I would have to take the initiative if I did not want to spend my evenings at home alone. Some of my widowed friends were satisfied seeing women friends for lunch, meetings, and card games and then eating leftovers at home alone in the evening; but I was not. I was busy during the day, alone at my desk most of the time. I wanted to see people in the evening. I had not only Helen but also Kathy as role models.

Kathy surprised and impressed all her friends after Bub's death, when she began inviting couple friends to dinner. While Lev resisted letting her pay the tab, we knew she would not feel free to call us unless we allowed her to reciprocate. Her hospitality kept her connected to her old friends, and her example served me well in my new role as a widow learning how to entertain alone.

Though some old friends faded away, a world of potential new friends was out there waiting for me. Especially as that first Christmas and Valentine's Day approached, I wanted to surround myself with other women who were alone, who understood my loss. I sat down and listed every single woman whom I knew well enough to invite to my home—a grand total of nine. I asked them over for soup one Sunday evening in December and then to an "unValentine party" on February 14. I covered my large coffee table with hearty snacks and served good wine while we watched a comedy about a woman of a certain age—Meryl Streep in *It's Complicated*, I think. Another widow in the group followed suit and invited us to her condo a month or so later. That was the beginning of my new circle of friends. I met other women through them; and as the years passed, other old friends, including Phyllis, joined us in the sisterhood.

Women were incredibly easy to entertain, because food was simply an excuse to get together. We were not trying to impress one another, and my days of wanting to be the next Julia Child were over. I could serve Mexican food, a big pot of soup in the winter, salad in the summer, wine and cheese before a concert, or coffee and dessert afterwards.

Lev had been my partner in entertaining, willing to pick up a forgotten item on his way home from the office, bartending, carving the meat, washing dishes afterwards. As a widow I needed to simplify, to reduce the workload. Cooking, as well as cleanup afterwards, was much easier for four or six than for eight or twelve. While most men did not fit comfortably around my breakfast table, women happily gathered in that intimate circle. I found the courage to put my gold-band china in the dishwasher. Despite all the warnings when I married, the gold did not tarnish and the plates did not shatter. I put away the Waterford crystal and invested in less fragile stemware. I closed the bar and bought good wine.

While I occasionally invited couples to a restaurant or private club for dinner, I found it awkward for everyone. Like Lev, the men had difficulty allowing a woman to pay. Rather than cause a scene fighting over the bill, I usually acquiesced. I decided it was easier to entertain at home. As time passed, I grew increasingly comfortable mixing couples and single women at my dinner table. Since the meal was generally more complicated and the group larger when men were present, I depended on my housekeeper to help me in the kitchen. Rarely, I hired a caterer.

As my confidence grew, I occasionally hosted buffet suppers for two or three dozen—large enough to invite people whom I might not know well enough to ask to a seated dinner, such as younger couples and new widows, but small enough to use my own dinnerware and linens.

Using my own things, sharing them with friends, and cooking for others brought me great pleasure. I loved my home, but I was far happier when it was filled with people than when it was empty. Entertaining gave me a reason to pull out my wedding gifts, replace the burned-out lightbulbs, clean the house, and weed the garden. It also gave me a reason to cook again. At one time, I was considered an excellent cook, serving as coeditor of *Fiesta*,[1] a top-selling community cookbook. Now I was back in the kitchen, concocting new recipes and experimenting with old ones. With cooking as with gardening, I resumed a long-forgotten hobby.

Like many widows, I found that my social life slowed down on weekends when my married friends spent time with their spouses and other couples. A Sunday night supper filled that hole: Friday, grocery shopping; Saturday, getting the house in order; Sunday, cooking. And an invitation for "Sunday supper" conveyed the idea of casual and simple. Friends with full social calendars were most likely to be free on Sunday, while most widows were glad to have a social event to anticipate, to end the weekend on a high note.

On a very different scale, a widow in Amarillo addressed her dread of coming home from the family gathering on Christmas Day to her empty house by having an annual multigenerational open house on Christmas night. She stayed busy all afternoon getting ready for her party—no time to brood or wallow in self-pity—and her party became the hottest ticket in town.

In Corpus Christi, Chela did much the same. One of the first of her friends to be widowed, she soon began reaching out to other "strays." Her famous New Year's Eve dinner—an evening of fancy dresses, sparkly jewels, and champagne toasts—started with a handful of friends with nothing else to do and grew through the years to number almost one hundred. I was honored and grateful when she invited me on my first New Year's Eve after Lev died.

Lev and I became acquainted with Chela and Jimmie when Lev went into business with Jimmie's brother Ralph in 1975. Jimmie, a pioneer in offshore oil drilling, met Chela when he was working in South America. She was the privileged daughter and niece in a family of Italian winemakers who had immigrated to Argentina. She moved to Corpus Christi in 1961 when she and Jimmie married. The attractive, sophisticated blonde with her distinctive Spanish accent and beautiful clothes was a glamorous addition to the South Texas landscape. Though Jimmie and Chela did not have children, she embraced his children, his parents, his siblings, and their families. They became her family. Corpus Christi became her home.

Chela and Louise first reached out to me when they attended Lev's memorial service—a ministry of presence that deeply touched me, given our very casual connections. Along with their close friend Maureen, they have been consistent, reliable friends ever since.

I did not know Maureen and Bill as long or as well, but Lev and I were repeatedly the recipients of their hospitality when they opened their spacious, waterfront home to community groups. Maureen and Bill and their two children moved to Corpus Christi from the Midwest in the early fifties. Bill, too, had a successful career in the oil business. All my friends wanted to look like Maureen—always impeccably and elegantly dressed, her beautiful white hair always in place.

After Bill died in 2007, Maureen proposed that she and Chela should start going to dinner at the yacht club on Friday evenings. That was a brave act, and at first they endured patronizing comments about "girls night out." However, in short order club members took their presence for granted. Louise joined the group after John died, and over the years they included me and other single women. Those dinners became a high point of my weekends.

While no one needs to feel like her home is too small or her budget too modest to entertain, each of us has our own style. Some of my friends rarely, if ever, entertain at home; but they regularly buy tables at benefits for local charities. Those are coveted invitations. Other friends simply "make things happen." They are the ones who call to go to a movie or an art opening or meet for dinner. Some will include me on the guest list for big celebrations and major life events. Still others are present for their friends when they are needed. They bring soup and run errands for the sick. They drive friends to the airport and the doctor's office. In a variety of ways, they signal that they highly value their relationships.

C. S. Lewis wrote that joy has two components—memory and anticipation. In *Surprised by Joy*, he described "an unsatisfied desire which is itself more desirable than any other satisfaction. I call it Joy, which is here a technical term and must be sharply distinguished both from Happiness and from Pleasure. Joy (in my sense) has indeed one characteristic, and one only, in common with them; the fact that anyone who has experienced it will want it again."[2]

Business consultants Randall Stone and Dan Clay agree: "Happiness researchers find that upwards of half of someone's happiness is built in moments of anticipation and remembering. Happiness is as much about how we look forward to and look back on an event as it is about the event itself."[3]

As widows, we can live on our memories of the past, or we can create opportunities to live with joyful anticipation—always one more thing on the calendar to look forward to.

When we throw a party, we share that gift of anticipation with our friends. We can take those very events that are our sinkholes—holidays, anniversaries, even long weekends—and turn them into keenly anticipated and enjoyed moments. And as we practice hospitality, we create new happy memories for ourselves and for others.

✾

Lesson learned: In extending hospitality to others, we nurture strong relationships that enrich our lives and the lives of those around us.

Maturity Brings Wisdom

15

And Again, Joy

Finally, my brothers and sisters, rejoice in the Lord. To write the same things to you is not troublesome to me, and for you it is a safeguard.

Philippians 3:1

A portrait of my great-great-grandmother Aurelia Smith Davis Ripley Smith Woodward hangs in the Cabildo at Jackson Square, New Orleans, part of the Louisiana State Museum collection. Neither Aurelia nor the artist was famous. The primitive painting hangs to illustrate a widow in lavender half-mourning attire in the mid-nineteenth century. Aurelia's third husband and my great-great-grandfather, the father of her two children, was murdered in 1851.

Though Queen Victoria wore black for decades after her husband died, Victorian custom only demanded that a widow wear black for a year and a day before she could begin to wear gray and lavender—a period known as "half-mourning." Today, American widows have no obligations to observe a formal mourning period, and many choose to wear bright colors— even at the memorial service—to chase away gloom and sadness. However, some widows seem never to move from that period of grief and loss. They live with their memories rather than in joyful anticipation of all that life still has to offer. They remain in a lavender world of half-mourning. Or, in my friend Beverly's words, "They stay at the pity party."

Lev's last months exhausted me—a brief warning trip to the hospital in November, a Christmas that I was sure was his last, the 911 call on New Year's morning, followed by a month each in hospitals in Corpus Christi and Dallas. I thank God that Lev came home in early March with a reasonably good prognosis. He saw family and old friends, went back to the office and out to dinner. He bought a desk, anticipating that he might need to work from home occasionally. He even bought a new car four days before his death.

When he died quietly at home, we were all surprised by the timing; but his cardiologist had told me more than two years earlier that his congestive heart failure would probably lead to death within three years. Not until later did I realize that I had spent those years under constant stress. Stress, tension, and anxiety were my norms. Now I felt a guilty pang of relief and release that the other shoe had finally dropped, that Lev was freed from his long and heroic fight.

Like most "women of a certain age," I colored my hair for so many years that I did not know what my natural color was. During the months of Lev's final illness, I found myself repeatedly canceling hair appointments due to one crisis or another. My appearance was at the very bottom of my list of priorities. By the time I looked closely at myself in the mirror again after his death, I saw that I was very gray. Acknowledging that I was halfway to the stage that I would eventually reach, I decided just to go gray. Three months later I met my son in London at the end of his family's trip celebrating their older son's graduation from high school. Lev IV's first words were, "Mom, you're gray!" When I chided him for his not-so-tactful greeting, he said, "I don't like change."

If only my gray hair were the only change . . .

In my chronic exhaustion, I snacked between meals and sought energy from soft drinks at lunch. I gained ten pounds. Uncomfortable in bright colors, I avoided the bright reds, blues, and yellows in my closet and began to wear gray and shades of purple for the first time. Though I did not consciously try to dress appropriately as a new widow, the muted colors matched my somber mood.

I was surprised a few months after Lev's death when people started saying, "You look younger." "You look happy." Neither was true, but I recognized that I was under such chronic stress for so long that the tension showed up in my face. With Lev's death, that anxiety was gone. New responsibilities and big decisions created new anxiety, fear, and stress; but they were intermittent, rather than continual; and medication prescribed by my doctor helped me relax.

That first Christmas I avoided Santa Clauses and bright red; but I put up the tree and decorated the house with angels, evergreens, and white poinsettias. To have ignored the Season would have made it ever so much more depressing, my home that much emptier. I surprised myself as I hung the ornaments on the tree. Lev and I collected ornaments all the years of our marriage, picking up small items—not necessarily designed as ornaments—on trips around the world, and we frequently gave each other special ornaments on our December 16 wedding anniversary. Now, every ornament brought back a happy memory: the little red lantern that Lev had received as a child, the last unbroken hand-blown glass ornament from a set we purchased on our honeymoon at Sanborn's Drugstore in Mexico City in 1962, the hand-carved wooden bird we bought on the steps of the Papal Palace in Avignon in 1969, the glittery sand-cast plaster molds of Lev IV's and Peggy's feet from long-ago kindergarten projects.

While my weekends were empty, my weeknights were busy throughout December. I attended every Christmas event I could find—clubs, neighborhood, nonprofit organizations, church. I observed our wedding anniversary—a tough marker every year—with dinner one night with Peggy and Scott and the next night with Jo and Richard, who also had a December anniversary. I pulled out my Christmas china and linens for a birthday dinner with couple friends early in the month. I sent out an invitation to single friends that "Soup's On" the Sunday night before Christmas.

Just as Lev and I had done, our children always celebrated Christmas at their homes, grandparents invited; and we all gathered to open gifts under my tree and enjoy my traditional Christmas dinner at some point during the holidays, working around Lev IV's schedule—first as an Air Force officer and then as a commercial airline pilot.

Sensing that I dreaded the gap between Christmas Eve with Peggy's family and the big family get-together at my house on the twenty-eighth, Cheri proposed that I join her and the boys in Colorado Springs on Christmas night to surprise Lev IV, who was overnighting there between flights. Peggy, Scott, and the girls stayed in town with me, rather than going to their ranch, where Lev and I traditionally spent Christmas Eve with them.

On Christmas morning, anticipating the gathering of the entire family in three days, I emailed everyone a Christmas Decree:

> Whereas, Grumps personified the spirit of Christmas with his generosity, merriment, and love of all things Christmas; and
>
> Whereas, he exhibited that spirit in his collecting and giving of noisy, gaudy Christmas decorations and toys; and
>
> Whereas he further exhibited that spirit in the wearing and giving of Christmas ties, as well as the wearing of Christmas shirts from plaid to print, Christmas socks, and even Christmas pants of red plaid, patchwork, holly sprigs, and candy canes, and *always* a bright red blazer;
>
> Be it hereby resolved by his family, heirs, and friends to honor his memory by perpetuating his joyous celebration of Christmas; and
>
> Be it further resolved to banish all that is pretentious, sophisticated, stuffy, and somber from Christmas gatherings and celebrations; and

Be it further resolved that while an occasional, grumpy "Bah! Humbug" is permissible, the spirit of generosity, hospitality, and joy shall erase any tendency toward stinginess, misanthropy, or sadness; and

Finally, be it hereby decreed by the reigning matriarch and dowager that all black, brown, gray, purple, lavender, and other drab, somber colors shall be banned from all Christmas celebrations; and that celebrants shall be properly attired in all that is merry and bright.

This decree is effective immediately.

When Peggy and her family left Christmas afternoon to join Scott's family for their celebration in a nearby town, I flew to Colorado Springs. The Broadmoor was festive with Christmas lights reflecting on snow-dusted evergreens, excited children in their red velvets and plaids, doting grandparents hovering nearby. Even without Lev, it was a magical place for me.

Cheri and the boys returned with me to Corpus Christi two days later to prepare for our annual family celebration, and Lev IV arrived the next day. We were painfully aware of the empty chair at the dining room table, as well as in the living room, where Lev—our Santa—passed out all the presents piled under the tree. Peggy and Cheri knew that I would have fewer gifts under the tree, and they splurged on a gray coat with a fox collar for me. I passed Lev's Santa hat on to Lev IV. We laughed a lot, cried a little, remembered joys of past Christmases, and celebrated being together. It was our first step in a continuing experiment in how to do Christmas without husband, Dad, and Grumps.

What I did not realize then was that traditions and rituals are part of the glue that holds families together. Our tendency is to abandon those traditions because the empty chair is too painful a reminder of our loss. I now am convinced that traditions and rituals are more important than ever after loss. I have heard too many friends say, "Our family used to be close, but after Grandma (or aunt or mom) died, we drifted apart. She was the one who got us together."

As new friendships developed with other single women, I observed how they coped. One year Mary Anne turned her townhouse into a Christmas fantasy and invited all her friends—single and couples—who were spending Christmas alone to come for Christmas Day. She set up small tables in every available inch of space, pulled out her best china and silver, and spread out a feast for us. It was my first Christmas dinner away from family. To my surprise, I had fun.

With more intentional planning, I could have created more moments of joy in my early years of widowhood. Now, I make a practice of imagining and dreaming during the fall. *What do I want my house to look like when the family gathers to celebrate? Whom do I want to spend time with in December? What are my favorite, happiest Christmas activities?*

Then I appraise ugly realities. *What business/responsibilities/obligations cannot be postponed? Where are my sinkholes? What events and dates are emotionally threatening?*

I make a personal Advent activities calendar. I try to plan at least one moment of joy for every day, spreading out the onerous chores as much as possible and avoiding overcrowded days. My anniversary merits special care. Each year Christmas is better.

❀

Lesson learned: Finding joy, especially at those times when the empty chair is painfully obvious, is difficult but possible. It requires careful advance planning, intentionality, and enlisting family and close friends for support.

16

Beware!

Beware of the dogs, beware of the evil workers, beware of those who mutilate the flesh! For it is we who are the circumcision, who worship in the Spirit of God and boast in Christ Jesus and have no confidence in the flesh—even though I, too, have reason for confidence in the flesh. If anyone else has reason to be confident in the flesh, I have more: circumcised on the eighth day, a member of the people of Israel, of the tribe of Benjamin, a Hebrew born of Hebrews; as to the law, a Pharisee; as to zeal, a persecutor of the church; as to righteousness under the law, blameless.

Philippians 3:2–6

High on my list of new stress triggers were the betrayals by those who tried to take advantage of me. More experienced widows warned me, "Your time will come." Almost every widow I know has stories to tell, most—but not all of them—involving money.

A number of years ago I sat next to an older widow on a plane returning to Corpus Christi. Handsome, erect, with a strong jaw and steel-gray hair, she was a generation older than I. Our paths crossed occasionally, and I knew her children slightly. She told me that shortly after her husband died, his best friend called and invited her to dinner. Thinking he was very kind and thoughtful, she accepted. To her shock and dismay, at the end of the evening he expected to be invited into her home and into her bed. She never went on another date.

I assumed hers was a unique betrayal, but other widows have shared similar stories. They warn us to beware. Lecherous old men exist. An old family friend drops by unexpectedly early in the morning before you are fully dressed. He just "happened to be in the neighborhood." The friendly kiss on the cheek somehow lands on your mouth. Wandering hands drift out of bounds during a casual hug or under the table. We learn to be cautious.

I suppose I learned the lesson well, for I was spared that kind of humiliation. At the top of my list of betrayals and disappointments were my experiences with some of Lev's professional advisors and business associates. They presented themselves as friends during the many years that they benefited from the fees he paid. Lev IV repeatedly warned me, "Mom, these people are not your friends."

Joyce Carol Oates called them sharks. In her memoir of grief, she wrote:

> With the acuity of sharks sensing blood in the water, vulnerable prey thrashing about heedlessly, in the weeks and months following Ray's death many strangers—alas, not only just strangers—write to me with requests that begin with the inevitable/identical/heart-stopping words *I know that you must be terribly busy but . . .*
>
> *I know that, deranged with grief, no doubt suicidal and in many cases exhausted and not in your right mind, you might be prevailed upon to do a favor for me whom you scarcely know—but hurry!*
>
> Sometimes I am fooled—"fooled" is the apt term—by a letter that purports to be sympathetic *So sorry to have heard about the death of your husband* but is soon revealed to be a request for one or another favor. . . .
>
> How like predator sharks these seem to me! How I resent them! . . . Sometimes I am so upset, I pace through the house striking my fists together lightly, or not so lightly. I try very hard to imagine how Ray would react, if he were here to advise me.[1]

My first shark attack was from Lev's bank a week after he died. The second came about a month later, in a letter much like those Oates received. A purported friend, who had filed a lawsuit against Lev over a piece of junk property, offered to drop the lawsuit in exchange for an exorbitant amount of money, many times the value of the lot. Next was Lev's personal attorney, in a series of small, self-serving actions.

Lev had a five-year contract for a fractional share of an airplane, necessary for travel with his decreased mobility. It was a luxury I neither needed nor could afford. Instead of renewing the contract, I chose to terminate it. I was offered a buyback amount far less than what Lev had been told to expect. As he had with the lawsuit, Lev IV stepped in to help me. A pilot himself, he knew the actual value of my share, and he knew an aviation attorney qualified to challenge the offer. I dodged another shark attack.

A few years later, when I prepared to sell my remaining interests in Lev's old partnership, I offered the leases to men with whom Lev and Ralph had invested for decades. They were happy to take them off my hands, but for a price that was a fraction of their value. Luckily, my son-in-law Scott knew the oil and gas business and was familiar with online auctions. He helped me auction my interests for more than ten times what "friends" had been willing to pay.

Other friends of Lev caught me by surprise when they asked me for donations to their favorite charities and chided me for not doing business with them. A distant relative called and wanted to borrow a significant amount of money. I ignored the first request and managed to stammer out reasons I could not honor the other requests. Fortunately, I was not a person who had much trouble saying "no" through the years.

After Lev died, too many people wanted to tell me what I should do and how I should do it. I was never called on to be so strong or to say "no" so often as in those months settling the estate. I had never had to watch after my financial interests before. Lev had done that. Now I had to be alert to recognize those who did not have my best interests at heart. Confrontations left me emotionally drained. I was no longer the smiling spouse, but I had not yet mastered the role of client.

Repeatedly, I felt like people underestimated me, but I was fortunate to have knowledgeable family members, along with some friends and advisors I trusted. I went to them for advice when I had concerns about others' ethics. It would have been very easy for me to ignore nagging doubts and blindly trust Lev's old friends and associates.

At one point, I turned to Ralph, who was in his eighties, for counsel. He asked, "He's an old guy, isn't he?"

"Not really. He's about my age."

"That's old. Old guys think this might be their last deal and they need to make as much as possible. Young guys know that if they treat you right, they will have your business for life."

My family's trust levels were at a record low. In new business relationships, we were slow to trust, slow to let go of control.

But for everyone who tried to take advantage of me, someone else bent over backwards to be fair. My young oil and gas attorney apologized for his billable hours. He routinely told me how to do it myself, if I wanted to avoid his bill. Lev's real estate attorney accompanied me to the courthouse when I filed for probate. He charged so little in comparison to everyone else I dealt with that I told him his fees were too low. Our builder resisted charging me for routine repairs. Before I had time to call him, he and his crew showed up to board up my house in advance of a threatened hurricane. A used-car dealer not only bought Lev's beloved red Thunderbird from me, but he picked it up at Peggy and Scott's house, where I had stored it. I never had to physically deal with the car.

The betrayals were simply the worst of my unexpected losses. In addition to those who wanted to take advantage of me, many simply withdrew. In some cases, they were probably no different from me. Not knowing what to do or say, they stayed away. Just as Lev and I had not thought to mix singles and couples in our social life, not all our old friends continued to include me. In some cases, the magic of the relationship was gone. Lev had been the glue that held the four of us together.

Without him, we did not have much to talk about. And, of course, I changed—most drastically in those months of deep grief and overwhelming anxiety immediately after Lev's death.

Occasionally, people who I thought were friends proved not to be friends at all. I realized that we had been cultivated for business reasons. With Lev gone, there was no reason to continue to cultivate me. They were looking after their own interests, not mine. This wasn't friendship. It was networking.

Not quite so painful was the recognition that some were only crossroads friends. Our lives intersected at some point, and our friendship lasted as long as we were all at the same place. The relationship was based on activities and organizations that we shared in common. We had nothing deeper to maintain the friendship when we left the intersection to go in different directions. It could be couples whose husbands worked, hunted, fished, or played golf together. It could be a couples card group, Bible study, travel club, or dance club. Without the husband, the widow was no longer included.

Even when I continued to see married women friends during the day, I felt the loss of friendly relationships with their husbands. Conversations changed when men were present. Without Lev, I needed his male friends more than ever. Whom else could I ask about property tax, insurance, buying a new car, or repairing the old one? I was grateful for the handful of couples who continued to invite me to dinner and to their parties, for those who asked me to tag along on trips, for the men who talked to me as they had to Lev about investments, taxes, insurance, and the like. Almost without exception, I could depend on the men who had been Lev's closest friends through the years.

Jo and Richard were stalwart friends, meeting me for dinner almost weekly, having me to their house to "hang out" on weekend afternoons and evenings, visiting me in Dallas, traveling with me. Phyllis and Sam, who lived around the corner, always checked to see if I needed a ride to parties we were all invited to. Mary Ann and John had me to their condo regularly for home-cooked meals.

Clydell and A. C. were remarkable. Our friendship spanned more than fifty years. Once, their youngest son asked me, "Mrs. Prichard, how long have you been friends with my parents? I found black-and-white pictures of you." Chances are the photos were of early potluck Thanksgiving dinners together, when the men had only one day off work and we couldn't go home for the holiday. Clydell and A. C.'s hospitality and generosity were boundless. They continued to include me at their dinner parties and invited me to join them on a Baltic cruise and visit them in Carmel. They came to Dallas to take me out to dinner on my birthday.

Art Turock, corporate trainer and motivational speaker, has spoken of the difference between interest and commitment. In his description, a person who is simply interested will do a task only when circumstances allow; but a person who is committed to a task makes no excuses and accepts only results.[2]

This applies equally as well to people as to things. I need to be the kind of friend who is not merely interested but committed, responding to friends' needs whether it is convenient or not. I have not always been a committed friend. I tended to put my good works and my big projects ahead of relationships, but I learned that what may be a minor inconvenience or a small cost to me can mean an enormous amount to a friend. Now, nurturing relationships—making time for friends, spending quality time with them—is one of my top priorities.

❧

Lesson learned: We almost surely will encounter those who do not have our best interests at heart; but with God's help, we can find the wisdom and courage to resist them, while not allowing them to make us bitter or untrusting.

17

Priorities

*Yet whatever gains I had, these I have come to regard as loss be-
cause of Christ. More than that, I regard everything as loss because of the surpassing value of knowing Christ Jesus my Lord.
For his sake I have suffered the loss of all things, and I regard
them as rubbish, in order that I may gain Christ and be found
in him, not having a righteousness of my own that comes from
the law, but one that comes through faith in Christ, the righteousness from God based on faith. I want to know Christ and
the power of his resurrection and the sharing of his sufferings
by becoming like him in his death, if somehow I may attain the
resurrection from the dead.*

Philippians 3:7–11

Alice, who traveled this road many years before I did,
said, "Since losing my husband, I am a better person. I
am kinder, nicer, sweeter. I have my priorities in order. I know
what matters."

I had to agree. "Yes, you are. And so am I."

I could choose whether to be sad, angry, bitter, and self-
centered or thankful both for what I once had and what I now
have. I could control my thoughts. I did not have to throw a pity
party. As Eric Cantor said after he was defeated for reelection
as Republican Congressman from Virginia in 2014, "[While]
suffering is a part of life, misery is a choice."[1]

Like Alice, I reordered my priorities. I asked myself the
question: how do I choose to spend my discretionary time and

money? I examined my bank statements, my calendar, and my "to-do" lists. What did they tell me about my priorities? Did my priorities accurately reflect my professed values? Since my desk was never clean nor everything on my list checked off, I had to concentrate on what really mattered.

So much of what seemed to matter suddenly lost all importance after Lev died. *Loss of companionship*—what a simple phrase. Years later I still could not find the words to describe all the stomach-churning meanings and implications of the term. The danger was to let this void—this black hole—consume me.

Of course, physical and material things mattered. I could cope better because I felt safe and secure in my home, I had financial security, and my mind and body were relatively intact. I was one of the fortunate ones.

But all that paled in comparison to relationships. How many times through the years did I conclude a sympathy note with the wish that "you will find comfort from your family, friends, and faith"? So much of what I used to write I now considered trivial, if not downright offensive. But from personal experience, I can attest to the fact that family, friends, and faith were my support system when Lev died; and they continue to matter most in my life.

Family, undoubtedly, was my first priority. However, finding the balance of placing family first without suffocating them and always being available to them without demanding that they always be available to me was hard. My widowhood impacted my children's priorities. At this point in time, I now was on their list of responsibilities and obligations.

Mama was diagnosed with Parkinson's disease about the same time Daddy was diagnosed with incurable cancer. When he died, Lev IV was fourteen; Peggy, eleven. I asked Vernon, my longtime pastor, what my obligation was to my mother.

He replied, "Ella, you can't make your mother happy. What would make her happy would be to have your dad alive and healthy again and to have her own health. You can't give her that. You are responsible to see that her needs are met, but your first responsibility is to Lev, then to your children. That's biblical. Aging parents are like children. What they want and what they need are often two different things. You need to meet her needs but not her unreasonable demands."

Vernon, a biblical scholar, spoke from personal experience. His mother had moved to a retirement center in Missouri, and she was insisting that he or his brother move back to Missouri to provide a home for her. Every time I felt stretched or guilty or torn between my mother and Lev and the children, I replayed Vernon's advice in my mind. Through the years, I shared his advice with friends when they found themselves with conflicting family responsibilities.

Those little decorative pillows with clever sayings on them amused me. One in particular always made me smile: *Mirror, mirror on the wall/I am my mother after all.* Growing up, I never wanted to be like Mama. I very consciously emulated Daddy. Four years after Lev died, I finally realized that I was my mother. Vernon's words applied now to Peggy and me. If I could have one wish, the thing that would make me happiest would be to have everything the way it was. But Peggy and Lev IV could not give me that. Life is not a fairy tale. We do not simply marry and live happily ever after.

Friends mattered much more than things. Without friends, nothing else really mattered at all. I would choose poor health and a shorter life with friends over excellent health and long life alone, beans and cornbread with friends over champagne and caviar with strangers. Besides, by investing in friends— not only as unconnected individual relationships, but also as a community of older, single women with shared interests and values—I removed some of the pressure on my family to fill my hours and make me happy.

I wish I could list faith/God/church as my most important priority, but that would not be completely honest. My faith provided the peace and comfort that supported me through

Lev's death and that continues to sustain me today. However, as I told my pastor with some frustration more than five years later, "Jesus doesn't sit across from me at the dinner table." The promise that *I am with you always* (Matt 28:20) was a comfort in the abstract, but it did not fill the black hole of my loneliness or occupy the empty chair in my home.

I was surprised by the number of devout Christians and strong church members who, like me, did not feel at home—or even comfortable—in their church after their spouse died. Some were angry with God. More of us were simply ill at ease coming alone to a place where we were always half a couple, part of a family. For more than ten years, there were six of us in the pew for Sunday worship. Then Daddy died and Lev moved to the end of the pew. The children grew up. Now I am alone on the pew.

For most of my adult life, I served in the church—on committees, teaching teenagers, and eventually on denominational committees and boards. When Lev became ill, I drifted away from those commitments. I simply had nothing left to give. I never developed those traditional bonds that meant so much to my mother and her generation—the ladies' Sunday School class and the mission society. As a widow, I missed having a peer group in the church. I envied friends who found places of meaningful service and fellowship as widows. Faith is still on my list of "unfinished business."

Obligations to clubs and boards moved to the bottom of my list of priorities. I chafed at those calendar entries. I did not want my days dictated by meetings, though those meetings forced me to get out of the house and be with people. I tried to sort out which organizations brought me pleasure and which caused unnecessary stress. My rule of thumb was the same as I used in my business relationships: I liked those that made my life better, and I disliked those that made it worse. Eventually, I resigned from all but those less serious organizations, where the demands on me were low and I enjoyed the other people in the group.

Having been reared with the concept of the tithe—that nothing we have belongs to us and we give back to God ten percent of what He has given us—I was always committed to giving back. I went through Baylor on scholarships, the beneficiary of others' philanthropy, so giving back came naturally. As a middle-class, small-town girl, I found volunteer service the most comfortable way to be involved in the community as a newlywed. At least from the mid-seventies, Lev and I formed a terrific partnership in supporting the causes that we cared about. We loved making a difference. He had his passions, I had mine, and we supported them all.

At this new stage of life, I had to decide what to do on my own. On the one hand, I embraced his causes of black gospel music preservation and Baylor football; on the other, I decided not to continue support of some of the institutions that he loved, while I increased my support of the Colonial Williamsburg Foundation and began to support cultural organizations in Dallas and Nantucket. But responsible philanthropy takes work. It takes time. And for me, it is a growing priority.

I gave lip service to the importance of health and fitness; but for too long, I had no self-discipline when it came to diet and exercise. I had good intentions, but when my day was too full and something had to give, it was usually exercise.

During the years of Lev's declining health, I simply could not deal with my own wellness. We had more doctor appointments on the calendar than I wanted to think about, but it was more than a lack of time. I was worried about Lev. I coped by denying that I needed to take care of myself.

After his death, swamped with work, I did not have time to worry about myself. I saw my doctor about my anxiety—tight throat, tight chest, insomnia—but walked out of the cardiologist's office when I was sent there for an echocardiogram and stress test. I had flashbacks of all the times I had been there with Lev. For more than ten years, I watched the pounds pile on and did nothing, until finally the combination of vanity and bad knees forced me to consult a nurse nutritionist about my diet.

Keeping a food journal and checking in with the nurse every two weeks helped me develop good nutritional habits— low in carbs, salt, and fat; high in protein and vegetables. The program was realistic for the long-term. I have kept the pounds off, and—while not an exerciser—I try to include an hour of physical activity in my days: I walk, work in the garden, and tackle physically demanding household projects. I carry my groceries and lift my luggage. At my age, it is "use it or lose it."

But what about "Lev work"—my responsibilities overseeing the family business and the estate? I repeatedly filled free days on my calendar to the brim with "Ella work," only to have an unexpected business or legal issue force me to drop everything else to deal with it. With all my travels, I promised my advisors that I would stay accessible. I embraced twenty-first century communication tools, relying more and more on email and text messaging. I stayed connected via iPhone and iPad. I delegated what I could, in order to free time for the activities and people that I cared most about. When I began spending summers on Nantucket, I set up a home office there.

When I began writing, I added a new priority of solitude and reflection to my already overcrowded days. I restocked the index cards I had relied on as a new widow, once again creating daily timed agendas to carve out time to write, time for business, an hour for physical activity, and—ideally—time with friends. I learned to schedule the things that required mental energy and acuity in the morning and to move physical activity to late afternoon, when my brain was weary. I continually sought to find balance in my life.

✾

Lesson learned: Getting one's priorities in order—learning to do what must be done without neglecting what really matters in life—requires self-awareness, time management, and extraordinary self-discipline.

18

Maturity

Not that I have already obtained this or have already reached the goal; but I press on to make it my own, because Christ Jesus has made me his own. Beloved, I do not consider that I have made it my own; but this one thing I do: forgetting what lies behind and straining forward to what lies ahead, I press on toward the goal for the prize of the heavenly call of God in Christ Jesus.

Philippians 3:12–14

I have always been a perfectionist. Once that was a compliment, but now it is considered a disorder. I could be the only person in the class to pass a test, and my parents would ask, "Is it your best?"

Daddy constantly preached, "Anything worth doing is worth doing well." Mama conflated the parables of the ten talents and the faithful steward, often reminding me that *from everyone to whom much has been given, much will be required* (Luke 12:48b).

The King James Version, with which I grew up, constantly reminded me of the need to be perfect. The Apostle Paul's words were translated, *Not as though I had already attained, either were already perfect . . .* (Phil 3:12a).

Being the perfect daughter and student was not particularly difficult; so I was surprised to discover that being the perfect wife, mother, cook, housekeeper, friend, and volunteer—I was still trying to be the perfect daughter—was impossible. Nevertheless, my philosophy was that since nothing on this earth is perfect, everything can be improved.

Finally, my minister removed some of the burden of perfectionism when he preached on Christian perfection. Vernon explained that the Greek word for *perfect* means to be complete, to be mature. He used a pitcher as an example: "A perfect pitcher is one that holds and pours liquid as it was designed and created to do." It did not have to be a beautiful piece of crystal or one of perfect balance and scale. It merely needed to function as designed. That is what God requires of us—to be the women he created us to be, to be mature.

But what does a mature widow look like? I finally understood what an older, wiser friend meant when he told me, "You can't have wisdom if you don't have gray hair."

By the time I reached my fifties, I increasingly recognized that intelligence and wisdom are not the same thing. I began to suspect that the highly intelligent and highly educated may be the last to come to wisdom, for they can go far on knowledge alone. Mama often said, "He may be real smart, but he doesn't have any common sense." True, but wisdom is more than common sense plus intelligence. Maturity is a necessary ingredient.

As I searched for glimpses of wisdom in others, I realized that not everyone acquires wisdom along with gray hair. The wise habitually demonstrate good judgment and discernment. They tend to seek out those who are wiser than they are as mentors and role models. Their thought processes are logical, rational, and reasonable. They learn from experience and seldom make the same mistake twice. Of course, it is not an either/or situation. From foolish to wise is a spectrum. According to my friend Ralph, we all have "pockets of immaturity." Most of us probably have pockets of maturity as well. In the aftermath of death, as we learn our new role as widows, we need wisdom. We need to be fully mature.

I knew instinctively that I wanted to perform this role of widow well. Peggy complained that I overanalyzed everything, and no doubt I did, but that was how I kept my sanity. I studied to be a journalist and historian—a person who steps back, detached from what is going on, a spectator who analyzes the facts and the situations. Now, as a widow, I wanted to keep my emotions under control all the time, an impossible goal.

Widow conjures up sad, bad images of lonely old ladies, living on their memories, dependent on others to care for them. I could have meekly accepted the stereotypical role; or I could have tried to deny my new status, going about my life pretending that nothing had changed. Instead, I decided to embrace the word and the role and redefine them.

In writing my own script, I had clear images of both my mother and my mother-in-law as widows. My sweet Mama—who kept Lev IV for a month when he was two-and-a-half, played on the floor with him and Peggy, and let them bake mudpies in her good cake pans—was only seventy-three when Daddy died. Parkinson's disease had already taken its toll on her, and my children remember her as a semi-invalid in her seven years of widowhood.

In contrast, Helen, my mother-in-law, was widowed a second time when the children were toddlers. She was the merry widow, Auntie Mame, *grande dame*, and adoring Grandma and Granny-Great all rolled into one. We were not surprised when she married a third time. She and Bill spent twenty years traveling the globe, right up until the summer before she died. Even then she dressed every morning as she had for more than sixty years—in her girdle, nylon stockings, and high heels. To this day she remains a larger-than-life presence for all of us and an intimidating role model for me.

How will my children and grandchildren remember me? I was very conscious of the image that I would leave them. When I circumnavigated the globe to tour Hong Kong, Vietnam, Laos,

Cambodia, Thailand, and Sri Lanka in 2013, Peggy asked me to create a photo book for the grandchildren, so they could have a record of my climbing Angkor Wat and riding an elephant in Thailand. I doubt that Lev IV and Peggy will ever think that I have matched Grandma, but I have done my best.

Shortly after Lev died, I made a mental list of all that had happened in the forty-six years of our marriage. If I lived to my Aunt Adeline's age, I had another thirty-eight years to go. How could I productively fill so many years? It was not that I wanted to live to 106. If I lived that long, I wanted life to be as good as possible for as long as possible.

Former Baylor University President and Chancellor Ken Starr focused on joy in his December 2014 graduation speech. With references to Aristotle and modern psychology, he named three aspects of happiness: pleasure, a life well lived, and feelings of genuine commitment and active participation in community.[1]

A life well lived in community—that is a reasonable goal and expectation for mature widows. We need to live in community. We need a purpose for our lives. But I did not know how to achieve that in 2009. I was in search of meaning, community, and happiness.

While everyone advises widows not to make major decisions the first year, I made many important ones. Some, like changing advisors, were forced on me. Buying a condo in Dallas was not. I first broached the subject of a second home in Dallas in about 2006, but Lev said, "You've been smoking those funny little brown cigarettes again." Subject closed. However, a few weeks before he died, when we returned to Dallas to see the specialist who had overseen his care at Baylor Medical Center, he acknowledged that we might need to buy a place there, and he speculated that the timing was good. The Great Recession was a buyer's market. That was all the permission I needed after he died.

By fall 2009 I longed to escape the memories and the work that the house in Corpus Christi represented. I had moved the office home. I had selected new financial advisors. I was ready for a new project. My grandsons were growing up, and I wanted to spend more time with them. Since Lev IV's job as an airline pilot took him away from home several nights each week, I did not think I was fair to Cheri if I camped out with her repeatedly.

Dallas was full of old friends from Baylor and from Corpus Christi, and it was a great jumping-off place. While I no longer drove the 325 miles from Corpus Christi to Waco for Baylor events, I could easily drive the 100 miles down from Dallas. Texarkana, where I grew up and where I still had close friends, was 175 miles east. I could get just about anywhere in the world that I wanted to go from DFW Airport.

Guided by a Realtor who knew the market well, I started condo-hunting. I wanted the security and convenience of a high-rise condo in the section of Dallas where my family lived and that I knew best. I expected the search to take many months; but by my second trip, I had a good idea of what I wanted. I found a complex one block west of my route from Lev IV and Cheri's house to Baylor Medical Center. The building and its location would have been perfect for Lev. I sensed his blessings. I closed on February 4, 2010. After extensive remodeling, I moved in that September.

I chose a calm, serene "ladies' house party" décor—four single beds—completely different from anything Lev and I had ever lived in. We liked bold primary colors and solid, sturdy French country furniture. Now I surrounded myself with pastels and flowers, peeling veneers, and rickety English Regency-style furniture. For the first time, I furnished a home from scratch. Every dish, pot, pan, knife, sheet, and towel was new. I covered the bedroom walls with English prints and began the process of finding paintings for the living room. And the only person I had to please was myself.

Five minutes south of me was the Dallas Arts District, home of the symphony, opera, theater, and three museums. Having never lived in a large city, I had limited exposure to great art and music. Since Lev and I always supported Corpus Christi cultural organizations, I did the same in Dallas. I had no idea how much the arts would nourish my soul. I soon found myself planning my year around the opera and symphony schedules. Corpus Christi friends enjoyed coming up for long weekends of art, music, and shopping. I never visualized inviting couples to visit me, but I discovered that couple friends also enjoyed staying with me. Unfortunately, few of the men could sleep comfortably in a narrow twin bed. Eventually I adopted the European hotel solution. I pushed the twin beds in the guest room together so I could make the bed with king-sized sheets when couples visited. I even hosted family Christmas gatherings at the condo.

I pushed myself far out of my comfort zone. Not every new experience was one that I wanted to repeat. Not every new acquaintance became a friend. In some ways I was like a teenager. No one else could tell me what would work for me. I had to experiment and find out for myself through trial and error. I had to take risks. I never knew how I would react until I was in the middle of a new experience. When I found myself in an uncomfortable situation, I retreated.

Many of the books and blogs I read advise new widows to avoid social occasions while they are still emotionally fragile. Widows post, *Please understand why I turn down all your invitations. Please keep asking me. Someday I will accept.* I think that is a terrible idea for most of us. Isolation is a breeding ground for depression and contributes to a decline in mental and physical health.[2] Helen was right. When we keep saying "no," people forget about us and move on. We all tend to extend invitations to people whom we think will say "yes." That is one reason the sisterhood is so important. We can fall apart in front of our widowed friends. They understand, and they help pull us out of the sinkholes.

Today, my life is an adventure. I do not know what tomorrow will bring. I hope—I want—to react positively, but I still occasionally surprise myself by falling into sinkholes and tripping over the bumps on the path. I recognize my irrational overreaction when I stumble, but I cannot seem to stop myself. I need to say "I'm sorry" too often. I still need a lot of grace.

However, I keep pushing on. If I stay in my comfort zone, who knows what I might miss? This is a journey—probably my final act. When the curtain falls, I hope it will be said about me, "Well done."

🌺

Lesson learned: We become the mature women God intended us to be when we refuse to linger in the past but move into the future with optimism, courage, wisdom, and confidence.

19

Confidence

Let those of us then who are mature be of the same mind; and if you think differently about anything, this too God will reveal to you. Only let us hold fast to what we have attained.
Philippians 3:15, 16

Katherine Graham, who became publisher of *The Washington Post* at age forty-six after her husband committed suicide, described her confusion, fear, and lack of confidence that first year in her autobiography, *Personal History*. Her education, wealth, and social position did not equip her for her new role. She described how overwhelmed she was. "Sometimes you don't really decide, you just move forward, and that is what I did—moved forward blindly and mindlessly into a new and unknown life.

"Left alone, no matter at what age or under what circumstance, you have to remake your life."

She was terrified without her husband, insecure making decisions. ". . . all that Phil had been made my job more difficult. His having done everything so well—and, as it seemed to the world, so effortlessly—made it even more daunting to me. . . . I certainly didn't feel in any way equal to running the *Post* the way he had run it. . . . I had come to realize that I could only do the job in whatever way *I* could do it. I couldn't try to be someone else, least of all Phil.

"What I essentially did was to put one foot in front of the other, shut my eyes, and step off the edge."

Graham's experience was not unique. She could be describing me, though both her family and business responsibilities were incalculably greater than mine. Her children were twenty, eighteen, fifteen, and eleven when their dad died. Her mother was still living. And she inherited controlling interest in a Fortune 500 company. She had to learn the business, learn whom she could trust and rely on, and learn how to relate professionally to the executives who surrounded her. She had to give herself permission to manage the newspaper differently than Phil had. She, too, had a long list of "firsts."

"In any case, all those firsts during that first year of my working life added up, and I began to realize that just by putting one foot in front of the other I was actually moving forward. Despite all the inner turbulence and confusion, and despite my feeling unsure that life could really go on without Phil, my days were becoming more endurable and even, at times, interesting again."

Despite her mistakes and insecurities, she learned the business. She was at the helm when *The Washington Post* broke the Watergate story. Her autobiography won the Pulitzer Prize. Katherine Graham built a remarkable career and life in the thirty-eight years she was a widow. Her greatest regret was that of many other young widows, including my mother-in-law: that in remaking her life, she neglected her two boys still at home.

As she approached her seventy-ninth birthday, she concluded, "Fulfilling work, writing, keeping up with my old friends, adding new ones—these are the things I concentrate on now, as well as relating to my children and their families. My children remain remarkably close, even when they are having differences with each other or with me." Hers was a life well lived.[1]

On April 7, 2009, I was a different person than I am today. Like Graham, I operated in a complete fog that first month. I was tempted to stay in the fog, but I was not allowed to. Some things

I had to do myself. At first I simply went through the motions. People put paper in front of me and said, "Sign here." When Lev said that, I felt comfortable signing income tax returns and various legal documents without reading them. I never read them. I trusted him.

Perhaps it was the terrible timing of Lev's death. The stock market was sinking, and those complex exotic investments he had been talked into buying without fully understanding them turned to dust.

Perhaps it was the quick discovery that Lev's will and trust did not mean exactly what I thought they did. That simple boiler-plate language—*as the trustee from time to time considers necessary for the health or maintenance in reasonable comfort*—meant exactly what it said. My access to cash was strictly limited. During Lev's life we gave generously to our family and to charity. Despite repeated assurances that nothing would change when he died, I could not access principal for gifts, professional fees, taxes, or myriad other expenses. I had no confidence that I could continue to maintain the lifestyle I had enjoyed with Lev. I was entitled only to what was *necessary* for *reasonable* comfort. Even in the areas where I was permitted to dip into principal, such as home maintenance, I had to ask the bank trust officer for permission.

That got my attention, lifted me out of the fog of grief, and cleared my head. It made me doubly cautious . . . and less trusting, as well. I resolved that I would read and understand every document that I was asked to sign.

The drudgery of summer and fall—assuming the title of CEO of Prichard Oil Company, searching for a new bank, adjusting to the new reality of life without Lev—constantly exercised my gray matter and demanded every bit of left-brain analysis I could muster. My right brain was numb. Having to depend on my advisors and children, giving up control, allowing other people to know all my business, asking permission—which Lev never did—were hardest of all.

Through the years I observed older family members who, when they sensed they were losing control, fought harder than ever to maintain control where they could. They often turned on their unfortunate children who had to step in and take charge.

Lev's "aunt" was probably the worst example. His stepfather's sister had no living family to assume responsibility when her health failed. At the insistence of her doctor and friends, we moved her from a spacious apartment in an upscale retirement facility in Austin to an assisted-living complex in Corpus Christi. She never recovered from her anger. She changed her will to remove Lev as executor, and she accused me of stealing her fur coat when I brought it home for safekeeping. Lev faithfully visited her and listened to her tirades, but I chose not to subject myself to her abuse.

Even in close, loving relationships, I have heard horror stories of the parent—usually the widowed mother—turning on the child who is the primary caregiver. One friend asked her mother why she continually attacked her. After all, she was the one of three siblings who saw after her mother—paying her bills and taking her to the doctor, to church, to friends' funerals. "Because you are the one who is here," her mother answered. She was angry at her situation, and she wanted to vent. Being parent to the parent is tough on both generations.

I never want to be like that, yet I suspect that my occasional sharpness with my children and advisors was driven by my sense of losing control. I did not want them knowing my business and telling me what to do. Sol, my accountant, taught me how to maintain a little privacy while overseeing all these people I relied on to take care of me and my financial affairs: Don't let any one person know everything. Different advisors need different information, and your assistant only needs to know the part that you handle personally at home. Trust but verify. Learn enough to ask good questions. Keep honest people honest by paying attention.

Sol's advice worked. Thanks to QuickBooks, for the first time I knew the costs of running the business and the house. I learned to budget. It took almost two years for me to live within my means. I would like to think that a combination of the economy at the time and the enormous professional fees I had to pay to settle the estate was to blame; but the unpleasant, unexpected truth was that the division of the estate into various accounts reduced the amount of discretionary income available to me. So much for the lawyer's bland assurances that "nothing will change."

Nobody but Sharon needed to know the details of my personal expenditures, and she did not need to know about my investments or see my tax returns. I checked my bills and bank statements. I signed the checks. I read legal documents. I admitted my ignorance. I regularly interrupted to say, "Stop. Slow down. Explain it again. I don't understand."

I continued to pray for wisdom and discernment. During our bank interviews that first summer, I relied heavily on my children and advisors, assuming they would eventually reach a consensus about where we should bank and then make a recommendation to me.

On a trip to Chicago in August, as we listened to a brilliant economist extol the virtues of his firm's investment strategy, I had a moment of great clarity and certainty. I was overcome by a peace and assurance that I did not need to listen to any more of this. What I had heard the day before from another bank suddenly clicked. That institution's investment philosophy was very similar to Lev's. I understood it. I was comfortable with it. I felt God had heard my prayers for wisdom and discernment. I knew what I was going to do.

When we regrouped at the hotel at the end of the day, I did not need analysis from our attorney and accountant. I did not need to reach consensus with the children. I announced the bank I was going to do business with.

From that moment on, I began to acquire confidence. As my confidence grew, so did my willingness to let go of trying to manage everything myself. I learned to trust my instincts and my advisors. The degree of peace I felt proved to be a solid indicator of whether I was proceeding in the right direction.

I am glad I learned the oil and gas business and spent four years managing the companies. I can read monthly statements and ask intelligent questions. I still pay attention, spending several hours each week on business. I still need Sharon, but my life no longer revolves around the recordkeeping that management required. I have more time for friends. I have time to write, develop new interests in the arts, visit new places, and make new friends.

Without the need to talk business so often, the children and I enjoy one another more. Just as I separated "Lev work" and "Ella work," we have separated business and social occasions. We schedule quarterly meetings—usually by conference call—to discuss legal and financial issues, but business no longer dominates our conversations when we are together. We have adjusted to the new family dynamic. We have learned to live without Lev.

🔆

Lesson learned: As we develop confidence in our ability to meet our responsibilities with wisdom and discernment, we press on to the goal of being fully mature, accepting our circumstances, and living life well.

20

Role Models

Brothers and sisters, join in imitating me, and observe those who live according to the example you have in us. For many live as enemies of the cross of Christ; I have often told you of them, and now I tell you even with tears. Their end is destruction; their god is the belly; and their glory is in their shame; their minds are set on earthly things.

Philippians 3:17–19

If there is a book that teaches one how to be a widow, I have not found it. Well-meaning friends brought me devotional books about grief, death, and eternal life; but I did not need vague, warm, fuzzy platitudes. My faith was secure. Nor did I find prescriptive self-help books particularly useful. Oddly, many of those on the best-seller lists were written by males—professionals in the grief counseling business. Often, they had no personal experience with loss of a spouse. They offered theories and formulas and promised the impossible, like *10 Steps to Grief Recovery* and *12 Months to Happiness.*

Widows get too much advice—too many people telling them how to grieve, how long to grieve, when to make decisions, and when to move on. What works for one person may not work for another. There is no single right or wrong way to mourn the death of a spouse.

I had that mountain to climb that I had not climbed before. *How do I do it? What do I do next?* Yes, I had choices, as every widow does. I could reinvent myself. *But what kind of person do I want and need to be?*

In my desperate search for how to "do" widowhood, I looked for widows I wanted to emulate. I considered older family members. I recalled family stories. I thought of widowed friends and friends' widowed mothers, widows I had known in the church and in my volunteer work, and others who, in different circumstances, had overcome adversity to live with meaning and purpose. I also looked at widows who—like Katherine Graham—lost their husbands at a young age and went on to create productive new lives. How very hard it must have been for them. They had no peer group. Some were still rearing their children. Some had to go back to work for health insurance, if nothing else. If they could do it, surely I could.

Stories of widows—usually famous—abounded in the media, as well as in memoir, biography, even fiction; but I did not begin to read the literature of grief until almost five years later, after I started writing my own story. I found books by other widows beneficial because they capture the craziness and haziness of those first months. Like grief recovery groups, they normalize the experience of overwhelming grief. We learn we are not alone. We are not losing our minds. Our reactions are normal. However, many memoirs are based on journals kept during those first dark, painful months. Few offer the hope that life will be good again.

The stories of sudden, unusual, traumatic, and young death are more likely to be published; yet less than one percent of women under forty are widowed and under two percent of women between forty and forty-nine. There still was not a book for me until Diane Rehm published her memoir in 2016. Hers is the story of a seventy-eight-year-old woman, widowed after fifty-four years of marriage.

The longtime NPR host and journalist begins: "On June 14, 2014, my husband, John Rehm—age eighty-three—began his withdrawal from life. The aides at Brighton Gardens were instructed to stop bringing medications, menus, or water. His decision to die came after a long and difficult conversation the day before with [his physician]. . . ."[1]

John's quality of life had seriously deteriorated due to a long, losing battle with Parkinson's disease. Diane sat beside her husband's bed for ten days and watched as he starved himself to death. As I read her memoir, I had flashbacks of my parents' long, slow, cruel deaths (Mama's also from Parkinson's), rather than Lev's. Nevertheless, I was surprised by how many times I thought, *that's how I felt* or *that's what I did.* And while I will not become an advocate for the right to die, as Rehm did, neither will I judge her.

No one else is qualified to judge another's behavior in the aftermath of death. As Mama lectured me after a cousin lost her husband when the two were in their early thirties, *You can't judge until you have walked in her moccasins and slept in her tipi.* Most widows, having walked down the long road of grief, wearing the same moccasins, sleeping in the same tipi, are determined not to judge others who grieve.

Those of us who grieve identify with Rehm's guilt—her decisions to move John from their small Washington, D.C., apartment to an assisted living complex, rather than modify their home and hire round-the-clock caregivers, and to continue to work instead of becoming his full-time caregiver. We all have guilt and regrets. Rehm spent a lot of time looking back on her marriage, regretting the periods of stress and emotional withdrawal, regretting not spending more time with her children when they were growing up.

She eventually arrived at the place that most of us reach: acceptance, letting go of *what if* and *if only*, planning and repurposing her life "on my own."

Rehm had to figure out what would work for her, just as I did. Not all widows were positive examples. Most, in fact, were negative—images of who and what I did not want to become.

I thought of Mama and other older women in the church who were physically and emotionally fragile and who spent their years of widowhood in a sad, lavender, half-mourning, dependent state. I recognized that I was truly blessed to have decent physical, mental, and cognitive health.

My grandmothers were stark contrasts: Mamaw, so very sweet and loving, giving to family when she had nothing for herself; Mama Wall, fighting to the end.

Helen, my mother-in-law, widowed twice, lived life to the fullest, aging gracefully and maintaining her dignity even as she was dying. Mama, on the other hand, slipped into chronic depression and anxiety after Daddy died. Since she was a woman of deep faith, I was distressed by the change. I had never before seen any inconsistency between the way she lived her life and what she professed to believe. I asked Vernon, my pastor, about her inability to claim the promises of God and the joy that the Apostle Paul described, which she had taught me so many years earlier.

Vernon explained that depression is a physical illness, completely unrelated to one's faith. He cited a widow in the church who had successfully managed her husband's business and farm interests after his death and whose philanthropy had a significant impact on the church and the community. But throughout the last twenty years of her life, her depression was so great that she felt totally unloved, even by God, to the point where she doubted her salvation. I did not want to end my life like that.

I did not learn about *complicated grief* until much later, when Dr. Helen Harris introduced me to the term. While all bereavement is more complicated than outsiders can ever imagine and while recovery—that place where we are managing our grief instead of its managing us—is much slower, some people seem overwhelmed by grief forever. According to Harris, when the relationship is good, when your spouse is ill and you are able to say goodbye, recovery may take two to five years. When death is sudden, unexpected, traumatic or the relationship is troubled, widows are more likely to experience complications and may even experience clinical depression that lasts for years. They often need professional help to deal with the trauma and rebuild their lives.[2]

In searching for role models, I was subconsciously searching for new friend groups as well. I sensed that I needed to surround myself with widows whom I not only enjoyed but also respected—the kind of people I wanted to be. I had enough negatives in my new life. I wanted to be around positive, purposeful women. I sought role models and friends who maintained healthy lifestyles and who would encourage me to make wise, healthy choices. Widows are vulnerable, with few external controls and with temptations to engage in self-destructive behavior to escape the pain and loneliness.

Because my days were usually spent at my desk doing "Lev work"—and probably because this was our pre-dinner ritual at home—that time in late afternoon when I moved to the library, poured a glass of wine, propped my feet on the footstool, and read or watched the news was my signal to shift gears, relax, and transition to "Ella time." However, I remembered Helen's warning to her sister when she was widowed. "Never drink alone. I have seen too many friends develop a drinking problem after their husbands died." I did not want to become dependent on chemicals. I counted my drinks. I watched my medications. It was not just about living life longer. It was about living life healthier and happier.

Although I did not want my children or professional advisors to have the authority to tell me no, I needed them to be honest with me. Once again, I missed having Lev accuse me of "smoking those funny little brown cigarettes again." My freedom was liberating, but there were risks involved—and not only financial ones.

The goal simply to have fun can lead to a frivolous lifestyle without meaning at best, turning to chemicals or casual sexual relationships at worst. Due as often to ignorance about finances as to irresponsibility, widows can run through their life savings, so that they have inadequate resources to support them comfortably in advanced old age. It would be far easier for me to depend on someone else to take care of me than to muster up the self-discipline necessary to take care of myself responsibly.

Husbands like Lev worked hard so that wives like me had few demands on our time. Having to replace leisure activities with work at age sixty-eight was a shock. I finally found out what Lev did all day at the office, but it was too late to apologize for taking him for granted. My children were stunned by all my responsibilities. "Grandma didn't do this. Dad didn't intend for you to work so hard," they protested. They were correct. Lev expected me to have a life similar to his mother's. Circumstances required that I do much more.

My friend Emily observed, "Too many widows who were well cared for by wealthy, successful men pay big bucks to their lawyers and accountants to manage their affairs while they go in search of another man to take care of them."

Some of my friends, like my mother-in-law, found love again and in that love reclaimed joy. They wrote their final act with a new costar. They were not necessarily looking for someone to take care of them, but they found the companionship that all of us miss so dreadfully. Some remarried, but not all. They were fortunate. They were also the exceptions. Women outlive men, and the men our age generally are interested in women ten or twenty years younger. There are simply not enough good men to go around. As Chela so famously commented, "Most older men are looking for either a nurse or a purse, preferably both, and I'm not willing to be either."

I have lived long enough to know never to say never, but I am writing my script as a single. I am deeply indebted to the sisterhood—those single friends, both widowed and divorced, who welcomed me into their group, encouraged me, and showed me how to live. I decided that if I was going to make any sense of Lev's death, if any good was going to come from it, then I needed to walk beside friends who reached this act after me, to model that life can be full and rich, that it can have meaning. I can still make a difference.

❈

Lesson learned: By examining the lives of widows whom we admire, we can identify the attributes we need to move from grief to joy and choose the kind of widow we want to become.

21

Anticipation

But our citizenship is in heaven, and it is from there that we are expecting a Savior, the Lord Jesus Christ. He will transform the body of our humiliation that it may be conformed to the body of his glory, by the power that also enables him to make all things subject to himself.

Philippians 3:20, 21

After Daddy died, I noticed that giving Mama something good to anticipate was the surest way to lift her spirits. Whether it was simply looking forward to going out to dinner with the family or a major occasion such as Lev IV flying home from the Air Force Academy or her sisters-in-law driving down for a visit, she cheered up at the very thought of what was coming. She reminded me of a child waiting for Santa Claus.

Now I understood, for my spirits were also lifted by anticipation—the promise of the family or friends gathering, the celebration of some special occasion, or a trip to a special place. The planning filled my days with happy tasks. However, the danger of making plans was the enormous letdown when plans changed. I have never been known for my flexibility. If I was looking forward to a holiday with family, for example, and plans changed, my disappointment was so great that I found it difficult to conceal my hurt. I repeatedly fell into deep emotional sinkholes.

I often described our marriage as a perfect partnership, where I made the plans and Lev paid the bills. I knew what Lev liked to do and whom he liked to spend time with. After he died, I became more and more dependent on my family's plans for the Holidays, and I hated it. I felt like I had lost my job as mom. My unhappiness rubbed off on the children. Finally, in fall 2014, acting on Peggy's suggestion, I had the whole family around my Thanksgiving table again. I spent weeks planning the menu and days setting the table, grocery shopping, and cooking. I loved every minute. Knowing the plans far in advance and being in charge again completely changed my outlook on the Holidays. I approached Christmas with a joy I had not felt since Lev's health deteriorated.

After Lev's death, I consoled myself with the powerful imagery of him whole, well, and strong again in the presence of his Lord. Whenever my mind drifted to those dark images of his final illness, I willed myself to think of his joy in his eternal, perfect home. I anticipated seeing him again. I did not worry about the details—whether the streets are paved with gold or the gates covered with pearls, whether it is a spiritual or a physical body and place. I simply claimed God's promises.

My thoughts were hardly unique. Our belief system about God, physical resurrection, and heaven—whether we believe at all—affects our response when a loved one dies.

According to George A. Bonanno, a nonbeliever and psychologist who has devoted his career to the study of bereavement:

> How we think about the afterlife, if we think of it at all, almost certainly plays a role in determining whether we experience a continued sense of connection to deceased loved ones and, ultimately, how we cope with loss. . . . Each of the three major monotheistic religions, Judaism, Christianity, and Islam, in their most elemental form, includes some basic idea about a final resting place in heaven. . . . Under normal circumstances, such a benign concept

potentially soothes the otherwise savage dread we typically associate with death. In fact, highly religious people with strong beliefs about the afterlife generally report good mental health. They also report less worry and fewer anxieties about death. . . .

On the surface, the idea of heaven should be a comfort for bereaved people, at least during the initial period of mourning. For those who sincerely believe that heaven awaits the faithful, the death of a loved one is not a true good-bye. It is more like a prolonged absence, one that will end, eventually when the loved one and the survivor are reunited.[1]

The unexpected death of her husband compelled literary author Joan Didion to acknowledge that she did not believe.

I realized that I had never believed in the words I had learned as a child in order to be confirmed as an Episcopalian: *I believe in the Holy Ghost, the Holy Catholic Church, the Communion of Saints, the forgiveness of sins, the resurrection of the body, and the life everlasting, amen.*

I did not believe in the resurrection of the body.[2]

In contrast, NPR host Diane Rehm's belief—and the comfort she drew from her faith—is not too different from mine.

I'd like to think there is a heaven. . . . I want somehow to visualize something, however nebulous. I want to believe in the reports of those who say they've experienced some form of heaven, whether it's "the light" or a "presence" beckoning them. But I think my own idea of heaven goes beyond that. I want to believe that my husband has been reunited with his parents, has met my parents, and is with Jane, his godmother, who adored him. . . . My own belief, I realize, is rather childlike: they—all of my beloved relatives and friends now gone from me—are with John, and he is refreshed, he is new, he sparkles in their presence. He is without illness, as they are, and somehow each of them is engaged with all the others.[3]

Faith takes me beyond reason. If I could compile facts and evidence to prove the existence of heaven, I would not need faith. My testimony is very simple: God is good. God is faithful. God keeps His promises. I experienced God's faithfulness repeatedly through decades of my spiritual journey, even during my college years when I was disillusioned with the local church and filled with intellectual doubts and questions. Now, the memory of those experiences gives me the sure hope and expectation that God will not disappoint me in the future, just as He did not fail me in the past.

While my heart responded most to my Baptist tradition of low-church worship, gospel hymns, and evangelical sermons (preferably preached by PhDs), I found comfort in the liturgy of the burial of the dead, from the Episcopal Church's *Book of Common Prayer.* I preferred its Scriptures of hope and its focus on what God has done for and through the deceased to contemporary celebrations of life that too often seemed to resemble a roast more than a sacrament. We planned Lev's service as a worship service, starting with the Doxology—"Praise God from whom all blessings flow!"—and ending with the Hallelujah Chorus.

The Hallelujah Chorus from Handel's *Messiah* has stirred my heart for as long as I can remember. For more than fifteen years, part of my Christmas tradition has been to take an hour or two off from my hectic holiday schedule to play the *Messiah,* while I read the biblical Christmas story. My old sixty-minute CD ended with the Hallelujah Chorus, just like the church choir performances I heard over the years. After Lev died, I needed those "Hallelujah!" moments more than ever.

When I bought my condo in Dallas, I also bought season tickets to the Dallas Symphony Orchestra. On Palm Sunday 2011, near the second anniversary of Lev's death, I attended DSO's matinee performance of the *Messiah* with a world-class orchestra, magnificent organ, renowned soloists, and huge chorus. By the time the orchestra reached the Hallelujah Chorus I was sitting on the edge of my seat in anticipation. I thought it was the finale. But, no, that was the climax to the story of Jesus' birth. The story of His death, resurrection, and ascension was still to come. I hugged myself as the soprano sang, "I know that my Redeemer liveth." I broke out in chill bumps a few minutes later when the bass, accompanied by the trumpet, sang, "The trumpet shall sound, and the dead shall be raised incorruptible, and we shall be changed."

I experienced exhilaration unlike anything else since Lev's death. My ecstasy was so great that I could not face going back to my empty condo. I found a quiet restaurant nearby, where I reveled in my emotions and reread the lyrics in the program guide. I was flooded with Easter hope, and I celebrated Lev's life and death and eternal life.

That Palm Sunday experience introduced me to the music that moves me like nothing else—oratorios. Sacred Music. Jaap van Zweden, the Dutch-born music director of the Dallas Symphony Orchestra at the time, grew up with the sacred music of the church. The classical passions and requiems with orchestra, chorus, soloists, and organ were part of his repertoire. My memory of Palm Sunday 2011 continued to ignite my anticipation as I planned trips to Dallas to enjoy those magnificent performances.

In a very different way, my friend Louise claimed the power of anticipation as she spent weeks recovering from a broken pelvis in winter 2014. She loved opera, especially the Metropolitan Opera in New York City; and we already had tickets for three April performances. That was the carrot that she dangled in front of herself, the reward that motivated her to endure months of physical therapy. First, she worked to get back on her feet after weeks of bed rest. She avoided the trap of false pride and welcomed the freedom and security that a cane provided. We went to New York as planned, and she retired the cane shortly afterwards. With that success she looked for another carrot. She planned a trip to the Grand Teton National Park in Wyoming, where she and John once hiked. When her physical therapy ended, she scheduled regular workouts with a personal trainer. Seven months after her fall, she went on three hikes in the Tetons led by park rangers.

Her doctor admitted that when he first saw her after her fall, he thought she would never walk again without a walker. With determination, discipline, and her mind fixed firmly on her goals, Louise proved him wrong. Instead, she let success build on success. A year later, she added a trip to the Alps, where she had warm memories of annual hikes with John. The anticipation of and preparation for what would become annual hiking trips became strong, positive motivators for her to stay fit.

My attorney often said, "Respect the past; embrace the present; imagineer the future," referring to the Walt Disney Company term that combines *imagine* and *engineer*. As much as I loved my life as Lev's wife, I tried not to linger too long on my memories. I fully engaged in the present. Eventually I welcomed time alone to reflect, to daydream about the future, and to consider possibilities rather than think about loss, sadness, and fear. Like C. S. Lewis, I found that happiness comes from a combination of anticipation and memories.

❈

Lesson learned: Faith in a loving God who has promised an eternal, perfect destiny for His children gives us hope as we anticipate being reunited with our loved ones someday.

Peace Leads to Joy

22

Strength

*Therefore, my brothers and sisters, whom I love and long for,
my joy and crown, stand firm in the Lord in this way, my beloved. I urge Euodia and I urge Syntyche to be of the same
mind in the Lord. Yes, and I ask you also, my loyal companion, help these women, for they have struggled beside me in the
work of the gospel, together with Clement and the rest of my
co-workers, whose names are in the book of life.*

Philippians 4:1–3

Easter hope—or at least its exhilarating joy—was hard to
maintain in the face of death and all that followed. On that
Easter Sunday immediately after Lev's death, I was grateful to
worship with Lev IV and his family at the Church at Horseshoe
Bay, high up on the hillside overlooking Lake LBJ in the Texas
hill country. I was glad to be among strangers, people who did
not know I was grieving, in a place where Lev and I had worshiped on other Easters. Afterwards, the family headed back to
Dallas for work and school, but I spent the night there on the
lake by myself before driving home to face an empty house. I
was totally at peace that evening as I sat on the shore, wrapped
in a blanket, watching the sun sink slowly below the hills on the
opposite shore.

The four-hour drive back to Corpus Christi on Monday
morning bought me time to prepare mentally for what awaited
me at home. I resolved to be strong for the sake of my children

and grandchildren, as well as to honor Lev's confidence in me and to keep my sanity. I did not think I could afford to fall apart.

Unfortunately, ugly realities disturbed my fragile peace immediately, when the bank served notice that it would no longer do business with me as it had with Lev. That was not the only time I lost control, but it was the worst. The loss of the bank's assistance and expertise in settling the estate and my growing doubts about Lev's attorney added immeasurably to my stress and anxiety.

I had never before needed to be so strong, so tough. Lev had always been the "bad cop" in our marriage. Dispute with a service man? "Lev, handle this." Dispute about a bill? "Lev, handle this." I did not know how to move from smiling spouse to client with advisors whom Lev had considered friends. While I was surprised by the size of charges for travel and "research," I did not question them. I let them add up until my anger boiled over. Then I overreacted. I fired Lev's attorney in a terse email; and when he called for an explanation, I could not speak. I was unhappy with myself—with my inability to remain calm. After several encounters ended badly, I learned to ask questions and express disapproval more calmly, rationally, and quickly.

In those early months when getting out of bed and putting one foot in front of the other was a struggle, I found comfort in the words of the prophet Isaiah:

> but those who wait for the Lord shall renew their strength,
> they shall mount up with wings like eagles,
> they shall run and not be weary,
> they shall walk and not faint. (Isa 40:31)

We all want to soar like eagles; but in times of grief, it is a gift simply to walk and not faint. After Lev died, I recalled the sermon that John Claypool preached when his young daughter was battling leukemia.

> Who wants to be slowed to a walk, to creep along inch by inch, just barely above the threshold of consciousness and not fainting? That may not sound like much of a religious

experience, but believe me, in the kind of darkness where I have been, it is the only form of the promise that fits the situation. When there is no occasion to soar and no place to run, and all you can do is edge along step by step, to hear of a Help that will enable you "to walk and not be faint" is good news indeed. It not only corresponds to the limits of the situation, it also speaks to the point of greatest difficulty; namely, of being able just "to hang in there," to endure, to be patient, and not to give down one way or the other.[1]

I am not the only widow who has crawled back into bed and pulled the covers over her head, succumbing to grief, trying to forget all that needed to be done in the aftermath of death. Young widows told me that only the fact that they had to get their children off to school got them out of bed and on their feet. But I had no children or job to get up for. Why not linger at the pity party and let someone else take charge?

Instead, I took Sol's advice. Most of the time, I got on my feet and—step by step, day by day, month by month—I climbed that mountain. I survived the funeral. I filed for probate. I closed the downtown office. I cleaned Lev's closet and sold his car. I could say with Claypool, ". . . here I am this morning—sad, broken-hearted, still bearing in my spirit the wounds of darkness. . . . By the grace of God, *I am still on my feet.* . . . All I am doing is walking and not fainting, hanging in there, enduring with patience what I cannot change but have to bear."[2]

My growing emotional strength helped me pull the family together around a common purpose during our search for a new bank. After the hard work of settling the estate was complete and new advisors were in place, we gathered less often as a family. I missed that. While we had no significant disagreements, individual concerns, interests, and aspirations took precedence over family unity.

Later, when I looked back on that time period, I realized that I should have made a greater effort to continue family traditions and rituals that brought us together. My new attorney recommended annual family meetings to tell family stories, pass on family values, and strengthen relationships among the younger members of the family; but the grandchildren were only eighteen, sixteen, twelve, and ten when Lev died. I could not imagine what a family meeting would look like. I slipped into the practice of randomly seeing family members in smaller groups, grateful for every opportunity to be with them. Now that the grandchildren have reached adulthood, I am finally at the place where I can begin to visualize that annual family gathering. Another piece of unfinished business.

The family business, where Lev IV and Peggy served with me as directors, seldom required much effort or attention from the board. From the beginning, I told them I could not run Apco forever. I knew that I would not always have the physical energy or the mental acuity required. I calculated that by the time I was seventy-six, Lev IV would be eligible for retirement and Peggy's youngest would be in college. Living in two different places with two very different operating styles, they could not easily share management of a small company. I put them on notice. By 2017 one of them would have to take the four-drawer file cabinets that accompanied management. Neither of them wanted the job, and I had no intention of continuing indefinitely. I did not see a good solution.

At the time, I was serving on a university investment advisory committee, which was looking for a new investment manager. As bankers pitched their services to our committee, they described the work of their oil and gas divisions. I did not know that one could delegate management of mineral interests outside of a trust agreement. This sounded like an ideal solution for our family. I checked with my advisors first and then with my children. Thanks to Sharon and QuickBooks, I knew exactly what my expenses were to operate Apco. The bank's fees were significantly less. Everyone was pleased with the solution, Lev IV and Peggy most of all. Now they will never have to find room for the file cabinets. They will never have to argue or flip a coin to decide who will manage the company.

Selection of an outside manager solved our immediate problem, which so many small family businesses face after the founder dies; but it had potential long-term benefits as well, since undivided assets are often at the root of family conflicts.

In a family business, the one who heads the company often feels overworked and underappreciated, while family members who only profit from earnings sometimes believe that the manager is overly compensated. The head of the company may want to reinvest earnings for long-term profitability, while stockholders or limited partners want to maximize income. On the other hand, while it may seem logical to have all the children share responsibility equally, that can pit them against one another in a tug-of-war over how to manage the property or the business.

Even without a family business, undivided interests can cause problems. One child may be sentimentally attached to the family homestead or ranch, while another wants to sell it. Disagreements increase when the heirs have very different financial circumstances, with different needs and obligations. The family member who lives nearby and can move into the family home or enjoy the family ranch or beach house every weekend is more likely to want to keep it than the one who lives 1,000 miles away. Too often businesses and other family properties are sold or divided by court order because the heirs cannot agree or compromise.

A headline from the *Chicago Tribune* summarizes the fate of heirs to the founders of Hyatt Hotels. "Fortune's fate: Pritzker family agreement to divide billions in wealth comes to a close. Tumultuous 10-year effort to divide estimated $19 billion fortune, one of the nation's largest, ends, and many family members go separate ways."

In 1995 brothers Jay and Robert Pritzker wrote their ten children and a cousin, stating their wish "that the family trusts would be used to build the family's businesses and not be

tapped sources of 'individual wealth.'" They named Tom Pritzker, one of Jay's sons, to be in charge. And then Jay died. Within
a few years, family members began to question Tom's management and then to accuse him of transactions that benefited
his family—and, in some cases, two other family members—
instead of the entire extended family. After ten years of wran-
gling, the fortune was carved into eleven pieces, most of the
cousins left the family business, and some still do not speak.[3]

We are not a litigious family. We wanted to avoid law-
suits at all costs. We agreed that family harmony was far more
important than tax issues or the cost of administering the
estate. Part of my role as matriarch was to provide strong leadership for the family and to set an example of placing family
needs above my personal needs. I could not change Lev's will,
but I was determined to manage my own affairs in a way that
would strengthen the family, not weaken it. I want more than
the absence of strife. Above all, I want peace within the family,
both during my lifetime and after I am gone.

❀

*Lesson learned: We reclaim our strength as a family in times of
grief and crisis when we put aside our disagreements and stand
firm, presenting a united front to the world.*

23

Gentleness

Rejoice in the Lord always; again I will say, Rejoice. Let your
gentleness be known to everyone. The Lord is near.
Philippians 4:4, 5

No one would have praised my gentleness in those first
months after Lev's death. I had to reach down deep inside
to draw every ounce of strength and courage I could find. I
had never needed to be so analytical; but at the same time, I
had never needed to be so conscious of others' feelings and
reactions.

I once summed up the job of a news reporter as gathering
all the information and then laying it out for the public to read
without regard to the consequences, to let the facts fall where
they will. In my new role, I quickly learned that I needed to
weigh every word and to consider very carefully how my words
and actions would be perceived. I hated it! I hated having to
worry about others' emotions and reactions. I believed that
facts should be facts. To shade them in any way whatsoever
felt somehow devious and manipulative. I struggled to find the
balance between being completely clear and being courteous. I
had to learn to speak gently.

Sometimes my professional advisors' advice felt like high-
pressure salesmanship, and I instinctively pushed back. When
I sensed they were patronizing me, I was offended.

Lev made every advisor a friend, and he treated them like friends—with lots of locker-room banter—in their business relationships. I often heard him talking to them on the telephone. He might slam down his fist, utter an expletive, and let them know in no uncertain terms that he was not going to pay their bill. The next minute he would inquire about their family or share a joke. His anger dissipated as quickly as it erupted, and he never held a grudge.

On occasion, I longed to deal with people in the same way. At first I was too dependent on my advisors and too unsure of myself in my new role to challenge and question them, although at times I should have. Moreover, I was reared to be a lady in the old-fashioned, Southern sense of the word. *Ladies don't curse. Ladies have good manners. They are polite and say "please" and "thank you."* I did not need to act like a man in a man's world. To the contrary, I observed that most men did not react well to bitchy, bossy women in business or in politics. What was considered assertive in men was interpreted as aggressive in women.

I needed to remain a lady, a *gentlewoman* to borrow the archaic English term. At first I tended to ask deferential questions—*Please, will you . . . ? Can you . . . ? Do you mind . . . ?*—when what I meant was, *I want you to . . . Please do this . . .* I learned to be firm and direct, to disagree respectfully, and to communicate that in clear, declarative sentences.

Dr. Haim Ginott, a psychologist, was in many ways the Dr. Spock of the 1960s and 70s. His book *Between Parent and Child* was the guidebook that young parents consulted in disciplining their children. He stressed positive communication based on mutual respect. Instead of criticizing or attacking their children with a finger-pointing *you . . . ,* parents were to describe unacceptable behavior and their own reaction to it—*I want . . . I feel . . . .* Those techniques, which I cultivated when I was rearing my children, proved invaluable in my new role.

Though I developed a different style than Lev to relate to my advisors, I also copied one of the hallmarks of all of his relationships. I made an effort to know my advisors personally, to know something about their lives outside the office. I continued Lev's practice of asking about their families and sending baby presents and Christmas cards. Most were young enough to be my children, and I was genuinely interested in them. But it was also very much in my self-interest to maintain good relations with them and to be positive, affirming, and appreciative. I reminded myself to apologize when I was wrong or when I wasted their time—both frequent occurrences, especially in the early months when I still had so much to learn. I tried to respect my bankers' time especially, since they—unlike attorneys and accountants—were compensated by fees based on assets, not on billable hours. Conversely, I learned not to be chatty with those who billed by the hour.

My advisors knew I could be tough. I did not have to prove it with tough language. They knew I had replaced most of Lev's advisors and I could replace them. I could still be gracious and smiling—a "lady"—even if I was now the client instead of the spouse.

I also needed them to have gentle spirits. I was an emotional tinderbox, ready to blow up at any moment. I wanted a team of advisors who were collegial, not competitive. On the one hand, I needed assurance that they would be absolutely resolute in protecting my best interests. On the other hand, they "handled" me most effectively when they were low-key, soft-spoken, and easygoing.

Sol, my trusted accountant, advisor, and friend, was first among equals. Lev and his parents had been among Sol's first clients when he established his firm in 1975. I was among his last. He had delayed his retirement when Lev's health worsened, and he devoted most of his working hours to settling the estate after Lev's death. As I became more comfortable with my team, I began to notice that my new, young advisors sometimes pulled their punches, reluctant to disagree publicly with Sol's advice. His young partner handled my routine accounting and tax needs, but he did not step up as a full member of the team. I reluctantly acknowledged that the time had come for Sol to follow through on his retirement plans. I found it painful to initiate the conversation. Fortunately, I had learned a little from the dreadfully emotional, unprofessional ways in which I terminated my relationships with Lev's bank and his attorney. Our friendship survived, and he has remained available for counsel.

When I joined the Baylor University Board of Regents in 1992, I did not own a suit. Corpus Christi is a semi-tropical, beachfront resort town. Bankers and lawyers shed their coats and ties in the summertime. I was the fourth woman on the board, taking my place among forty-four men. Some of them headed Fortune 500 companies, while another was on the Forbes 400 list. They were my models for my board wardrobe—the much-maligned pantsuit—and for board behavior. The strongest and most successful among them were also Southern gentlemen of the old school—gracious, courteous, considerate, and gentle. And tough as nails where principles were involved.

Drayton McLane owned the Houston Astros when we served together. One day he complained that a mutual acquaintance in another city never said "thank you." When Drayton traveled to meet with him, he didn't thank him for coming. When he called on Drayton in his office, he never thanked him for his time. Drayton was quite the opposite—never too busy to send a hand-written note. More than ten years after we worked together, I still received occasional notes from him. From him I learned the importance of acknowledging others' good work, of thanking them for their time and effort.

Many years ago, Ralph, who was my mentor as well as Lev's partner and our friend, told me, "Ella, you're honest to a fault," with an emphasis on the word *fault*. He taught me how to be a friend:

- To have a friend, you have to be a friend.
- To have a friend, present yourself friendly.
- Sandwich criticism. When you must offer criticism, start with the "bread" of compliments or praise—find something good to say at the beginning and the end. The critical part is the "meat" in the middle.

I relied on email to communicate with advisors, family, and friends. It was perfect for sending a message to my attorney: *I need to speak to you about xyz when you have time. I'll be home all day tomorrow. When can you talk?* It was less than perfect for communicating problems and complaints, because by its very nature email is brief, informal, spontaneous, and not carefully edited. Sandwiching criticism and saying "please" and "thank you" were not the norms in email. Text messages were even riskier.

As a writer, I was far more comfortable putting words on paper, where I could say exactly what I wanted to say without argument or interruption. I liked to weigh every word, edit what I had written, and then give the recipient time to think about his response. I was far less comfortable in verbal exchanges, where I too often became shrill and emotional. Nevertheless, despite my personal discomfort, I grew increasingly convinced that face-to-face meetings were the most effective and least risky way to solve problems and resolve conflicts. I noticed that professional advisors and business associates were far more willing to share information verbally than in writing.

I once joined my attorney in his office for a conference call. I was fascinated by his body language during the call—when he took notes, when he leaned forward to hear every word, when his attention drifted to other items on the table. Those who participated by speaker phone could not possibly have had the same experience that I had. They missed important nuances. Another lesson learned.

In a very different arena, Facebook also taught me the importance of gently speaking the truth. I reluctantly joined Facebook in 2008 after I asked the oldest grandson for his prom pictures. He responded, "Gram, if you want to see my pictures, you need to friend me on Facebook." I was not going to turn down a friend invitation from my seventeen-year-old grandson. In fact, the grandchildren motivated me to learn to text message as well. If I wanted to communicate with them, I needed to master their technology and media.

After Lev died, I turned to Facebook to fill the communication void—the black hole—in which I found myself. One day I wrote with raw honesty about my emotional pain. My friend Kay commented, "Once again you speak painful truth." My goal was not to inflict pain on other widows. With my Facebook friends, as with my local friends, I needed to speak the truth lovingly and gently.

Pulitzer Prize-winning critic Sarah L. Kaufman observed:

> We're living in what I call the grace gap. We hurry through our days, with our eyes and ears plugged into our devices, our minds far away, not noticing the physical or emotional impression we make on others. Our impatient, fragmented, competitive society conspires in many ways against gentleness and understanding. Popular culture stokes delight in humiliation and conflict.
>
> We're in an environment of grabbing and taking: taking advantage, taking control, taking for myself. Grace, by contrast, is associated with giving. . . . Total dominion is the desired image to project. Power is valued over grace; taking is celebrated. Giving is considered a lesser quality, even a weakness.[1]

In contrast, the Apostle Paul advised the congregation at Philippi to be gentle and forbearing. He implied that they would find joy when they lived in harmony with others. He recommended an open, trusting, conciliatory attitude rather than one of petty bickering and faultfinding. Simply put, the community was better served when its members sought to strengthen their relationships rather than damage them.[2] This gentleness was not about being meek and weak. In the ancient world, gentleness was the virtue—Aristotle's golden mean—midway between the extremes of anger and indifference.

In my journey, I discovered that gentleness led to peace, and peace with others gave me an inner peace that opened my heart to experience the peace of God again.

※

Lesson learned: The logic is inescapable. Widows usually find that relationships bring us our greatest joy. Gentle, loving words and actions contribute to strong relationships. Therefore, developing a gentler nature—learning to bridle our tongues and control our tempers—will improve our relationships with family, friends, and those with whom we do business. We can be both strong and gentle.

24

Peace

Do not worry about anything, but in everything by prayer and supplication with thanksgiving let your requests be made known to God. And the peace of God, which surpasses all understanding, will guard your hearts and your minds in Christ Jesus.

Philippians 4:6, 7

When I deluged my Facebook friends with my observations on widowhood and my experiences in that role, some responded, "Keep writing." I had a book in my head, the book I wished that someone had given me when Lev died, a book to help widows through those first months of emotional turmoil. *Rejoice!* That was the word the Apostle Paul used over and over again, but the very idea of rejoicing in the face of death and loss was inconceivable, the very suggestion offensive. The joy had gone out of my life. I needed to reclaim joy if I wanted life to be good again.

New Testament scholar David Garland observed, "A thankful spirit crowds out selfish pride, checks fear, defuses anger, and directs one's thoughts outwardly toward others."[1]

In the years after Lev's death, I sought to live life in gratitude mode as I continued to pray for wisdom and discernment and for God's protection for our family. I experienced the truth of Garland's words. When at last I slowed down and let go of my worry and anxiety, I sensed the peace of God. After more than four years of frenetic busyness and travel, I was increasingly content with my solitary lifestyle.

After my brief, joyous visit to Nantucket in August 2013, I longed to return for an extended stay. I spent that next year evaluating my life and deciding my priorities before I returned to that tranquil island—to that sanctuary—to see if I had the discipline to write. If I could not write every day in that place so far removed from all my responsibilities and cares, then I could not write. If I could not spend extensive time alone in reflection and contemplation, then I could not write.

By spring 2014 I was planning the details of my upcoming visit to Nantucket and writing the outline of my book. I spent an hour each morning meditating on the Apostle Paul's letter to the congregation at Philippi, followed by forty-five minutes on the treadmill, where I continued to sort out my thoughts. Paul's letter contains four chapters. I carved each into seven sections that spoke to me. I cleared my old desk in my bedroom (not in the office where I did my "Lev work") and stacked up various Bible translations, concordance, thesaurus, index cards, and notebook paper. I printed out the words of the old hymn, "Speak to My Heart," to sing as a prayer at the start of each writing session. I meditated on Philippians—a section a day for twenty-eight days—reading it in the New English Bible and Phillips Modern English, as well as the New American Standard Bible, my choice for study and worship. Occasionally I returned to the King James Version, for that was how I had memorized many of these passages as a child. Next, I wrote in longhand on notebook paper whatever experiences I recalled, whatever insights I had that seemed to illustrate the passage. Those stream-of-consciousness notes—those vignettes of death and grief—formed the basis for my first draft.

Shortly after Internet genealogy software was developed, my cousin Bill provided me with a copy of his and his daughter's research on our family history. I had heard family references to origins in Massachusetts, but I knew no more than that. Our family stories revolved around Mississippi and Louisiana, the Civil War and Reconstruction, "cousin" Jefferson Davis, and the Lost Cause. Both sides of my family had long been Baptist. Imagine my shock to discover that our earliest American ancestor was the Rev. Henry Smith, a Puritan minister who came to America about 1636 and served as the "first settled minister" of the church in Wethersfield, Connecticut. Five generations later, in 1776, his descendant, the Rev. Jedediah Smith, minister at the Granville, Massachusetts, Congregational Church and a Tory, fled with his wife, ten children, his sister-in-law, and her two children to the British colony of Natchez, Mississippi. He died within a week of their arrival in Natchez, leaving his family to survive alone in the wilderness.

Fascinated by this surprising new information that I was descended from Puritans and Tories, I began to study the history of New England, the English Reformation, and American religion. Lev and I drove through Connecticut and western Massachusetts to visit those Colonial towns and churches where my ancestors had lived and worshiped.

On my 2013 Maine cruise, I viewed the simple, steepled Congregational churches in every village. Afterwards, on Nantucket, I visited its historic churches. But in all my travels, I never attended a Congregational worship service. That was one of my goals on my return trip to Nantucket the next year.

I stayed eighteen days on that second trip, writing three hours each morning. Five years, four months, and twenty-nine days after Lev died, I completed the first draft of my book— 30,000 words. I was finally able to write about a peace that leads to joy, because I found that peace on Nantucket.

Near the end of my stay, on an August Sunday morning as gray as Nantucket's old shingle houses, I walked up the gently sloping hill from my hotel to the First Congregational Church, established in the early 1700s, built in 1834, its tall steeple dominating the skyline.

I immediately felt at peace as I entered the simple, serene, neoclassical church. The shutters were open, and light streamed in through tall paned windows, supplemented by a single large brass chandelier. The sanctuary had no heat or air conditioning. A breeze blew through the open windows as the pianist played a prelude by César Franck.

The theme of the worship service was peace, and every element of worship focused on peace—the peace of God and prayers of peace for the nations. During the sermon, an associate minister took the children up the ninety-four steps to the bell tower. There, where they could see the entire island and the Atlantic Ocean stretching beyond to the horizon, they prayed in all four directions for peace for the world.

We read Scripture. We prayed aloud and sang hymns together. We passed the peace. A baby was baptized. We placed our offerings in traditional Nantucket lightship baskets. And then the senior minister, in his Geneva gown and stole, stood in the high pulpit to preach. We exited as the organist filled the sanctuary with Bach's transcription of Vivaldi's *Concerto in A minor*. In the narthex, church members served cookies, lemonade, and coffee.

I do not know if Congregational churches have changed much since my Puritan ancestors proclaimed the Word of God from their high pulpits in colonial New England, but I felt a strong connection to my roots. I shed my anxiety and found peace there. This was the first place, the first time where I could imagine being alone on Thanksgiving Day or Easter Sunday. This was not the same ecstatic joy I felt when I heard the *Messiah* on Palm Sunday 2011 or that I experienced when I explored Nantucket a year earlier. This was a quiet joy, where I could honestly say, "It is well with my soul."

After years wandering through a spiritual desert, I had found my soul's home. I left the church singing the old hymn:

> My faith has found a resting place,
> Not in device nor creed;

I trust the Ever-living One,
His wounds for me shall plead.

I need no other argument,
I need no other plea,
It is enough that Jesus died,
And that He died for me.[2]

As transformational as that Sunday morning was, it was only the first of many blessings that I received in community with that congregation—too many coincidences to be coincidental.

Leaving the church that day, I introduced myself to the children's minister, explaining that I was visiting from Corpus Christi, Texas. Excited, she turned to introduce me to Debra, the senior minister's wife, who was born in Corpus Christi.

With some audacity, I emailed Debra and Gary and invited them to join me for lunch at the hotel the next day. Despite the age difference, we discovered many connections. They had met in Waco, Texas, where they both worked at Word Inc., a Christian record company and publishing house, while he studied for his Ph.D. in religion at Baylor University, my alma mater. We had mutual friends. We became better acquainted as Facebook friends. By the time of my 2015 visit, we had bonded.

I decided to make Nantucket my summer home, and I enlisted Lev IV and Cheri to help me with my search for a house to rent. They rejected every house I looked at: I would have to carry groceries upstairs at the upside-down houses, with their second-floor living rooms and views of the water. The stairs at the eighteenth-century house were too steep and narrow, the walk to Main Street too far. Then the Realtor pulled up to the curb of a newly renovated 1838 Greek Revival house on Centre Street. I loved the house, and my children deemed it safe and appropriate for me. The street looked vaguely familiar. Debra and Gary's 1790 parsonage was three doors away, next door to the church. I could see the steeple from my back door.

My 2016 move from hotel to house, from tourist to summer resident solidified my love affair with Nantucket, my involvement in the church, and my friendship with Debra and Gary. Peggy called Nantucket "Mom's happy place," and it was. Some women go to destination spas to detox. Nantucket was my detox time, a place where I found it easy to maintain a healthy lifestyle.

The only stress producer on the island was traffic, when the population expanded by ten times in the summer. Without a car, I had no stress. Instead, I chose to stay near the historic center of the town, where I walked down cobblestone streets to the grocery store and fish market, shops, restaurants, museum, and library. I explored the historic neighborhoods that lay in every direction from late spring, when the roses were just beginning to bud, to midsummer, when the hydrangeas began to fade from the heat. I checked out the flower boxes that decorated almost every window. I turned a corner and stepped back into the seventeenth century. I never tired of the waterfront—the wharves, beaches, lighthouses, and all the boats from tiny dinghies and classic wooden sailboats to huge ferries and mega-yachts.

My diet was simple: fresh fish and seafood from the North Atlantic, produce from area farms, and pink wine—those fresh, young, light rosés from Provence. Bad food simply did not exist on Nantucket. I had more than twenty good restaurants, from simple diners and take-out delis to the smartest of smart casual, within a ten-minute walk. Sunset was late and the streets were safe.

At its heart, Nantucket is a small New England village. I saw the same women I met at the church at concerts, movies, charitable benefits, and Bartlett's Farm truck on Main Street. I never expected to be part of the community—that was not even a wish—but it proved far easier than big, busy Dallas, where everyone was always in a hurry and I seldom saw the same person twice. Nantucket is extraordinarily philanthropic, with benefits and festivals every weekend of summer. I quickly found charities that I wanted to support, where I saw the same Nantucketers repeatedly.

We all need a place that gives us peace and settled happiness, a place of both good memories and keen anticipation. For me that place was Nantucket, a sanctuary for me as it was for those New England dissidents who arrived in 1659, seeking refuge from Puritan harassment on the mainland. And though the Quaker sea captains and merchants who dominated Nantucket for more than a century are long gone, island values still reflect their pacifism, simplicity, and unpretentiousness. While I smiled at the t-shirts that proclaimed that "America is that large island off the coast of Nantucket" and at Nantucketers' references to "going to America" when they left the island, "America" seemed very far away and inconsequential when I was there. I lived in the present. I was at peace. And I was overwhelmingly grateful.

❀

Lesson learned: When our hearts are filled with gratitude, we have little room for immobilizing worry, anxiety, fear, and misunderstandings. Letting go—turning them over to God—exposes the soul to the peace of God, which is the first step to reclaiming joy.

25

Attitude

Finally, beloved, whatever is true, whatever is honorable, whatever is just, whatever is pure, whatever is pleasing, whatever is commendable, if there is any excellence and if there is anything worthy of praise, think about these things. Keep on doing the things that you have learned and received and heard and seen in me, and the God of peace will be with you.

Philippians 4:8, 9

In the months after Lev died, I had no peace. During the day I controlled my negative thoughts by staying very busy. When I started to feel sorry for myself, I remembered friends who were optimistic despite great personal difficulties. I made mental lists of all that I had to be thankful for. I recalled happy memories to drive out unhappy ones. I did not allow myself to replay images of Lev's final illness and death or to dwell on *what if* and *if only.*

Once I made peace with myself, I needed to seek peace with those I loved most. That began with me. I needed to be a person who was true, honorable, just, pure, pleasing, commendable, excellent, and praiseworthy. I needed to dwell on these things, speak about these things, read books about these things, and watch movies and TV about these things. And I needed to associate with others who did the same.

Lessons from the past guided me in my new role. When I was a teenager, our senior minister was forced to resign after church leaders withdrew their support. Mama did not approve, and I never forgot what she said. "I have loved every pastor I ever had. I thanked God for their strengths, and I prayed for their weaknesses."

Every person, every organization, every community, and every government body has both strengths and weaknesses. No one is perfect. We can discipline our minds to find the good. We can focus on what we have in common instead of on where we disagree. When everyone else is tearing down, we can build up. To sit silently in a gripe session infers agreement. We can contribute a positive word to the conversation without becoming argumentative.

Because I was a perfectionist, I was critical too often when others' efforts were less than the best and goals aimed too low. More than once, someone said sarcastically, "Okay, Ella, tell us what you *really* think."

By 2002 I was aware that my critical nature, coupled with my directness, was not helpful in working with a group. I wrote on a card, which I kept in my Bible:

My commitment:
- Persistent in prayer;
- Intentional in encouragement;
- No negativism;
- Constructive in criticism.

While I certainly was not totally successful in changing my attitude, my written commitment reminded me regularly of my good intentions. I focused most on being an encourager. Lev IV made me aware of how poorly flight attendants were treated by passengers, if they were even recognized as human. I resolved to make eye contact whenever I could, to greet them, and then to thank them at the end of my trip, no matter how bad or how late the flight was. Next, I focused on the checkers and sackers at the grocery store—again, eye contact, personal greetings, and "thank you"—wishing them a nice day before they had time to wish me one. With practice, I began to make eye contact with almost everyone with whom I came in contact, to smile, and to say "thank you" for every small service and act of kindness.

While chattiness and friendliness came naturally to many of my friends, I was painfully shy among strangers. This was a difficult step for me, but it served me well in my new role as widow. Whether dealing with those with whom Lev had always dealt previously or entering a room of strangers alone, I pretended that I was comfortable by smiling and making eye contact. As others responded to my effort to present myself friendly, my attitude changed. My shyness diminished.[1]

In those first weeks after Lev died, I stared at my calendar, overwhelmed by the absence of any personally satisfying activities, even human interaction. Evenings were especially lonely and difficult, so I began to spend Sunday afternoons planning my week and filling my calendar. I ensured that I had something special on the calendar every weekend, preferably almost every evening. I followed my mother-in-law Helen's example and resolved to accept every invitation. I wanted to earn the reputation for always being available.

Before Lev's death, I never paid much attention to the length of days, the hours of sunlight. During the long daylight hours of summer, I felt free to go to restaurants, malls, and theaters in the evening without worrying about dark streets and parking lots. Unlike most parts of the country, fall in South Texas held the promise of a break in the heat, when we could enjoy being outside for exercise and sports, gardening, and entertaining. Even on the shortest day of the year, we had more than ten hours of daylight.

However, fall became a major source of stress for me as a widow. I dreaded the end of Daylight Saving Time, when nightfall arrived before six o'clock. That period from early November to December 21 was the most difficult period of the year.

I felt trapped at home by the darkness. My sense of aloneness increased. For friends who no longer drove at night, the feeling of isolation was even greater. For the first time, I marked the Winter Solstice. While it was the shortest day of the year, it also reminded me that Christmas—with all its hope and joy—was just around the corner and that the days would begin to grow longer again.

I needed light. For months I left the lights burning throughout the house day and night, until at last my soaring electric bills brought me back to reality. Dark places, dark books and movies, people with dark moods and thoughts depressed me and kept me awake at night. I wanted to be surrounded by beauty and serenity. Too much color and too much clutter set my nerves on edge. I sought books, movies, and plays that made me laugh and that had happy endings. The fine arts—both visual and performing—became a major source of pleasure and provided new opportunities for socializing.

In the first sixty-eight years of my life, I suffered from depression only three times: when I was twenty-five and Daddy was diagnosed with prostate cancer; thirteen years later when he was diagnosed with multiple myeloma, an incurable blood cancer; and in 1995–1996, when I broke my foot and was confined to a wheelchair shortly after my mother-in-law was diagnosed with an inoperable brain cancer. In each case I was powerless to change the situation. When Helen was dying, I changed my response. I engaged in intense, regular prayer and meditation, where I found the peace of mind that I so desperately needed.

Losing Lev was completely different. My whole life changed overnight, and it could never be the same again. I would never be the same again. For the first time, I was truly alone. At the same time, I was unbelievably busy. While I did not plunge into clinical depression, I was despondent. Because I had to deal with so much that was difficult and discouraging, small incidents that I once could have ignored sent my spirits plummeting. Some days my thoughts were trapped in fear and anxiety, and I wallowed in self-pity. I tried to avoid complainers, fault-finders, and gossips. Their negative attitudes were poisonous. They left me emotionally drained and depleted.

My attitude improved and I was a more cheerful, positive person when I surrounded myself with people who enjoyed life, who remained optimistic about the future, and who were involved in making the world better, instead of complaining about how bad everything was. I wanted friends like Phyllis and LaRae, who saw the good side of almost everyone and every situation. Like me, they were willing to go out in the evening with other women. They still traveled. They still looked ahead with anticipation, making plans for the future. Their laughter and enthusiasm were contagious. They did not live in the past—no lavender half-life for them. When I was with them, I had hope for my future.

Phyllis embraced life with all its fullness. Her every experience was a good one. When the conversation turned into gossip, she gently changed the subject or challenged the gossiper with a question, *How do you know?* She never found fault with a friend or family member. My secrets were safe with her. Though her husband, Sam, battled cancer for many years, they never dwelt on illness, and they continued to travel the world as they always had. He died in 2012, three weeks before they were scheduled to join me in Williamsburg with two other couples. Phyllis came alone. She confessed much later that her first stay in a hotel room by herself filled her with loneliness and isolation, but she presented a brave and positive front during a busy week filled with sightseeing and parties. She made every effort not to cast a shadow of sorrow on our time together.

LaRae was always filled with laughter, always ready for a new adventure. She personified the attitude *don't sweat the small stuff.* She laughed when I backed into her car in my driveway one night—a true test of friendship. When she learned that I had never been to Las Vegas, she was determined to take me.

She never said "no" if she could say "yes." Her spontaneity and flexibility were examples to me.

Perhaps I was fortunate to be older. Young widows have many additional issues to deal with, and their journey from grief to joy can be much more complicated. The *Wall Street Journal* reported that emotional well-being peaks when people reach their seventies. Their moods improve, partially because "older adults focus on positive rather than negative emotions, memories and stimuli. . . . They tend to prioritize emotional meaning and satisfaction, giving them an incentive to see the good more than the bad."[2] By this stage, most of us recognize that life is a gift, and we are grateful to be alive.

I still missed Lev and all the time we spent simply talking to each other. For decades my days began and ended with him, and now I found myself with far too few people in my life who shared my interests and concerns.

The virtual community proved to be an important outlet for me. For months after Lev died, I screamed my pain in anonymous tweets, hashtags *widow* and *grief.* I posted my first short essays on widowhood on Facebook. I could always find someone out there in cyberspace to respond and encourage me. I began to follow others who grieved. They shared resources, and their blogs showed me new ways to cope with my loss. I could encourage those who came after me—new widows whose cries in the night were not too different from mine. I found a supportive grief community.

Through Facebook I stayed in closer touch with my extended family, second-grade classmates at Fairview Elementary School, Corpus Christi friends who moved away, leaders in Baptist life across the nation whom I had met on some committee or board in the past, and scores of friends from Baylor—my roommates, coworkers on the student newspaper, and faculty, as well as administrators and other former regents. I nurtured relationships with new acquaintances in other cities. I shared newspaper articles that Lev and I would have discussed over morning coffee. I posted photos from my trips. I engaged in stimulating debates about religion and public affairs. Living in the very red state of Texas, I found more diverse ideas and opinions among friends on both coasts. I learned how to block and "unfollow" those whose crude, vulgar, angry, and racist posts offended me; and I learned quickly not to accept invitations to "friend" men who were strangers with no mutual friends. There are some creepy people who troll social media.

Imperceptibly, I began the long, slow journey to acceptance.

※

Lesson learned: To sense the peace of God continually, we need to fill our minds with that which is true, honorable, pleasing, and worthy. We need to fill our time with people and activities that promote healthy attitudes. Most of all, we need to model these virtues in all our relationships.

26

Acceptance

I rejoice in the Lord greatly that now at last you have revived your concern for me; indeed, you were concerned for me, but had no opportunity to show it. Not that I am referring to being in need; for I have learned to be content with whatever I have. I know what it is to have little, and I know what it is to have plenty. In any and all circumstances I have learned the secret of being well-fed and of going hungry, of having plenty and of being in need. I can do all things through him who strengthens me.

Philippians 4:10–13

As a college student I dreamed of going to New York and writing editorials for the *New York Times*. I wanted to change the world. Then I met Lev and freely abandoned my dreams. I moved to Corpus Christi and became involved in my new community.

A college friend who had followed his dreams asked me, "Any regrets?" referring to those dreams.

"No," I replied without hesitation.

"Why not?"

I told him about my Aunt Ruby and her Bible.

When I visualized my mother, the first image that always came to mind was of her with her worn Bible across her knees, index cards and pencil at hand, preparing her Sunday School lesson. I pictured her sitting in her chair in the den at night while Daddy read the evening paper and listened to the radio (and later watched television), at the Laundromat while she waited for her washing to be done, or at the kitchen counter when she took a break from her household chores.

Mama, a school teacher, began teaching a young women's Sunday School class at our church when she was in her early thirties, and she taught continuously for forty years. I once calculated that she spent twenty hours a week studying and preparing her weekly lessons. She was a serious Bible student, and to this day she is the primary theological and doctrinal influence on my life.

Those were the days of the Uniform Lesson and the six-point record system in Southern Baptist Sunday School: points earned for attendance, being on time, studying your lesson, bringing your Bible and your offering, and staying for worship. With the Uniform Lesson, all ages studied the same Scripture every week, though age-graded "quarterlies" contained different age-appropriate commentaries and practical applications. As in every other area of my life, Mama expected me to score 100 all the time. Virtually every night until I went away to college, she came into my bedroom carrying her worn Bible to read and discuss the daily Bible reading—one-seventh of the upcoming Sunday School lesson. I realized later that she developed her adult lessons from our bedtime conversations.

Her old King James Version Bible was falling apart, the spine of its cheap leatherette cover peeling off, pages spilling out. But she treasured it because it had belonged to her beloved Aunt Ruby, a spinster who spent her entire life on the family farm in southern Mississippi. On the flyleaf of her Bible Aunt Ruby had written, *Whatsoever state I am, therewith to be content. Philippians 4:11.* After she died in 1945, her bachelor brother Rod, who lived on the farm with her, gave Mama her Bible.

Mama must have introduced me to that verse and to the Apostle Paul's letter to the church at Philippi shortly afterwards, because it was a verse, a family story, and a lesson that I could not remember ever not knowing. It was the verse that has made widowhood bearable, even good.

Aunt Ruby's page-one obituary in the Magnolia, Mississippi, newspaper on February 22, 1945, provided a succinct summary of her life.

> Miss Ruby Roberts,
> Beloved Magnolian,
> Passes Mon. Evening

> The death angel visited the Roberts home just east of Magnolia on Monday evening at 6:30 and bore away the gentle spirit of Miss Ruby Roberts, one of the community's most beloved Christian women. . . .

> She was 73 years old, and was the daughter of the late Mr. and Mrs. John Roberts, a devout Christian couple who came to this community about fifty years ago. Miss Ruby was born in St. Helena Parish in Louisiana before coming to this vicinity. The family lived a few miles west of Magnolia on what later became the Lenoir place for ten years, and then moved just east of Magnolia and established a home, where Mr. and Mrs. Roberts lived with their large family until their deaths. There Miss Ruby and her brother, Mr. Rod Roberts, have lived ever since.

> Miss Ruby was a fine Christian character, and it can truthfully be said that a Good Woman has gone to her reward. She was a devout member of the Magnolia Baptist church, which she joined about fifty years ago. She had a quiet and unassuming manner, but she accomplished much good by her ministrations to her family and friends. . . .

Ruby was the oldest of thirteen children, the one ordained to stay home and help her mother in the house and garden and chicken yard. She helped tend the younger children from a very early age. Though five married and moved away, the others never left home. She cooked, cleaned, washed, and cared for them and her aging parents until—one by one—they died, and only she and Rod remained.

Mama loved the farm and spent as much time there as possible when she was growing up, taking the train from New

Orleans the day school was out each spring to spend the summer there. She persuaded her parents to allow her to live on the farm her senior year in high school.

I have vague memories of our last visit after Aunt Ruby's death. The old, unpainted house finally had electricity, and Uncle Rod was proud of the new electric stove. But the house still had no indoor plumbing, and I was introduced to the outdoor privy and taught to pump water. A dirt path led back into the woods behind the house, where the elderly cook lived in a shanty, which probably once housed slaves. The dairy, which provided a livelihood for the family for half a century, still had a few cows. The bull that serviced them was in a separate fenced pasture next to Aunt Ruby's garden and chicken yard.

Mama described Aunt Ruby as an intelligent, competent, loving woman. That single verse written on the flyleaf—*Whatsoever state I am, therewith to be content*—summed up her life. Through faith and focusing on others, she was able to accept her circumstances with grace and dignity. She was able to find a purpose, perhaps even a calling for her life. While she did not write the other key verse from Philippians 4 on the flyleaf, her life was evidence that she absorbed its meaning: *I can do all things through him who strengthens me* (Phil 4:13). Aunt Ruby did not claim to accept her narrow circumstances on her own strength. She understood that her contentment was a gift of God. In her faith, she found the strength to keep on keeping on.

After I began to dabble in genealogy, I drove back to Magnolia to learn more of the family history. I wanted to add facts to Mama's recollections. I went to the town cemetery and found the family plot where my great-grandparents and most of their children were buried, with simple, worn stones marking their graves. An elderly cemetery worker pointed out the road to their farm. Sixty years after my last visit there, I was sure I recognized the farm. I snapped photos with my smart phone and emailed them to an older cousin for confirmation.

These were my family roots. Mama absorbed the values lived out on that hardscrabble acreage and—in the Southern tradition of storytelling—taught me our family history and passed those values on to another generation. In the way her family lived their lives, in their calm acceptance of their modest circumstances, in their strength, in their hard work, and in their faith, they were unforgettable role models.

Alone in the early predawn hours after Lev's death, I picked up my Bible and reread Philippians. I claimed the promise for strength to get through the day. In the months that followed, I sought to live in gratitude for all that I had had and all that I still had. Very slowly I grew accustomed to solitude. Most of the time I was content—an acquired taste that did not come naturally. I had to work at it. Busyness, gratitude, and acceptance helped make contentment possible. Trusting God gave me the strength to move forward step by step, day by day, year by year. I was fortunate to have role models like Aunt Ruby. *How could I feel sorry for myself?* I had choices, opportunities, and privileges unavailable to earlier generations. I had forty-six years with Lev.

While outwardly my transition from wife to widow might appear less dramatic than the difference between a New York newspaper career and a traditional married woman's role in Corpus Christi, it was many times more difficult. I had no problem finding contentment as a young woman in love, establishing a home and starting a family. In contrast, finding contentment as a widow was a major issue. An older, more experienced widow advised me, "If you settle for contentment instead of happiness, you will be okay."

But I did not want to settle for less than happiness. I wanted my life to be more than merely keeping on keeping on. I wanted a purpose for my life. I wanted to reclaim joy. With God's help, I found the strength to accept my circumstances and to face the future with hope. And that laid the foundation for what returned so unexpectedly several years later—joy.

✸

Lesson learned: Our pretense of strength as new widows is the mask we wear to hide our weakness and vulnerability. Only when we acknowledge our discontent with our new role and admit that we are powerless to change our circumstances will we be ready to draw strength from our family, friends, and faith. Then we can find contentment.

27

Abundance

*In any case, it was kind of you to share my distress. You Phi-
lippians indeed know that in the early days of the gospel, when
I left Macedonia, no church shared with me in the matter of
giving and receiving, except you alone. For even when I was in
Thessalonica, you sent me help for my needs more than once.
Not that I seek the gift, but I seek the profit that accumulates
to your account. I have been paid in full and have more than
enough . . .*

Philippians 4:14–18a

If I learned one thing in the years after Lev's death, it was
that abundant living does not come from having more than
enough things. An abundance of things does not automatically
lead to contentment, generosity, and gratitude. It simply means
that we have plenty. Some people always want more. Others
simply shift their focus from getting more to keeping what
they have.[1] Sometimes abundance leads to pride and arrogance.
Having more than enough does not buy joy.

Instead, abundant living comes from an abundance of
good friends, meaningful relationships, and a purposeful life.
What I possessed materially proved not to be nearly so important or satisfying as what I gave away. Especially in those early
months, when I was overwhelmed by all I had to do to manage
Lev's business and settle his estate, giving away precious time
was perhaps hardest of all.

Weekends were especially bleak, so I welcomed the invitation to join Chela, Louise, Maureen, and their other single friends for dinner on Friday nights at the yacht club. That was my introduction to a marvelous tradition and to a marvelous new group of friends. In many ways it served as my initiation into the sisterhood—that common denominator of widowhood that bound us together because of our shared experiences of grief, loss, and building new lives alone.

Collectively and individually, these three women were a force to be reckoned with. They modeled for me a lifestyle of abundant living—having a purpose, making a difference, being a dependable friend. Their kindness and generosity were legendary. They continued to serve on the boards of the myriad charities they supported, sharing their time, talent, and treasure to enhance the quality of life for the entire community. They bought tables for almost every charitable benefit and graciously, generously invited a large range of friends and acquaintances to be their guests. They hosted charitable events in their homes.

When they became my friends, I discovered that their quiet, private acts of kindness and generosity far outnumbered their public good works. They taught me what friendship really meant. They lived alone without false pride. When they needed help, they asked for it. When others asked for help, they responded. Without children in Corpus Christi to call on in emergencies, they took care of one another. They took food to the sick, visited those in the hospitals, and attended funerals. When a younger friend went through a nasty court case, they were in the courtroom to support her. They reached out to every new widow they knew, just as they had to me. In enriching others' lives, they enriched their own. They intuitively grasped the value of enlightened self-interest.

They reminded me of my mother-in-law. When Helen reached her eighties, she noticed that her circle of friends was shrinking, so she began to invite younger women in her condo building to lunch. Louise, Chela, and Maureen did the same. As Louise said when she had another funeral to attend, "It's sad to see your old world shrinking. You have to keep your new world expanding."

Thoughtfulness was the key: thinking about others, thinking to include them, thinking to say "thank you," thinking to check on them when they were sick, thinking to be there with them and for them in the hard times as well as the good. In sum, it was about making relationships a priority.

Since this did not come naturally to me, I needed a plan to be more intentional about nurturing relationships. I jotted the names of sick friends on my "to-do" list. I stored birthdays on my electronic calendar, where I received automatic reminders. Whether by email, phone call, or hand-written note, I tried to say "thank you" for every kindness extended. Since I traveled frequently, I needed to reach out and touch base with friends when I was home. Otherwise, they didn't know where I was.

When time was short and my list included both pressing business and personal acts of friendship and kindness, I reminded myself to finish my "Ella work" first. If necessary, I would stay up until midnight or set the alarm for six in the morning to take care of essentials, but I knew that I would not do that to write a sympathy note or address a birthday card. If relationships were truly to be a priority, I could not relegate them to leftover time.

As I sorted out my priorities and sought effective ways to balance the "Lev work" and the "Ella work," I remembered Dr. Sidney B. Simon's Values Clarification—a trendy concept back when I taught teenagers in Sunday School. To help them determine what they valued most, I assigned exercises such as making lists of how they spent their time and money and with whom. If they could have one meal with a dozen people, whom would they invite? More than thirty years later, I found that I occasionally needed to perform the same exercises to

keep my life balanced and my priorities in order. Did my calendar and my checkbook reflect what I claimed was most
important to me?

I was naturally timid in social situations. My tendency was
to think, *Oh, those young women don't want to go to dinner with
anyone my age.* But I remembered how difficult life could be for
a younger single woman who had no peer group, and I recalled
how flattered I was when older women extended invitations to
me. I slowly gained the confidence to include younger women,
couples, and those outside my circle of "oldest, bestest" friends.
I tried to stay alert to women who were suddenly single, whether
by death or divorce. Once again I reminded myself that the
worst that could happen was that people might say "no."

I wish I could claim total success in acting on my good
intentions. More often than not, I failed to do all that I wanted.
"Lev work" got in the way. I fell in the rut of calling the same
few dependable friends to go to dinner week after week. Nevertheless, by writing reminders and making lists, I became more
sensitive to others. I got better at nurturing relationships. Regularly saying "thank you, God, for . . ." reminded me to thank
others for their kindness and generosity.

In recent years, psychologists and gurus in self-improvement
and positive thinking have studied and written about the role
gratitude plays in happiness and success.

Michael Hyatt, a prolific blogger on attitudes that lead to
success, examined Duke University's basketball coach, Mike
Krzyzewski, in "Why Giving Thanks Gives You an Edge." He
observed that the coach constantly emphasized gratitude.
Hyatt concluded that positive emotions like gratitude help us
become more resilient by giving us hope and reminding us that
we have agency. Most important, I think, "Gratitude moves us
into a place of abundance—a place where we're more resource-
ful, creative, generous, optimistic and kind. When we're operating from a place of scarcity, it tends to make us reactionary,
close-minded, tight-fisted, gloomy and even mean."[2]

Author and widow Judy Brizendine reached a similar con-
clusion in her blog on the crucial three-legged stool of gratitude,
hope, and resilience. She wrote, "When bad things happen and
life is difficult, gratitude may not be at the top of your list of
things to consider. But when you purposely stop and think of
what is still good in your life—and you begin to list the people
and things you're grateful for—your perspective changes. You
soon realize the many ways you've been blessed, both now and
in the past. And appreciating your blessings encourages you to
be hopeful about your future."[3]

But no one influenced me more than Sheryl Sandberg, COO
of Facebook and author of *Lean In*. In May 2016 she addressed
University of California, Berkeley, graduates on what she had
learned from the death of her husband.

> One year and thirteen days ago, I lost my husband, Dave.
> His death was sudden and unexpected. We were at a friend's
> fiftieth birthday party in Mexico. I took a nap. Dave went
> to work out. What followed was the unthinkable—walking
> into a gym to find him lying on the floor. Flying home to tell
> my children that their father was gone. Watching his casket
> being lowered into the ground.
>
> For many months afterward, and at many times since,
> I was swallowed up in the deep fog of grief—what I think of
> as the void—an emptiness that fills your heart, your lungs,
> constricts your ability to think or even to breathe.
>
> Dave's death changed me in very profound ways. I
> learned about the depths of sadness and the brutality of
> loss. But I also learned that when life sucks you under, you
> can kick against the bottom, break the surface, and breathe
> again. I learned that in the face of the void—or in the face of
> any challenge—you can choose joy and meaning. . . .
>
> One day my friend Adam Grant, a psychologist, sug-
> gested that I think about how much worse things could be.
> This was completely counterintuitive; it seemed like the way
> to recover was to try to find positive thoughts. "Worse?" I
> said. "Are you kidding me? How could things be worse?" His
> answer cut straight through me: "Dave could have had that
> same cardiac arrhythmia while he was driving your chil-
> dren." *Wow.* The moment he said it, I was overwhelmingly

grateful that the rest of my family was alive and healthy. That gratitude overtook some of the grief.

Finding gratitude and appreciation is key to resilience. People who take the time to list things they are grateful for are happier and healthier. It turns out that counting your blessings can actually increase your blessings. My New Year's resolution this year is to write down three moments of joy before I go to bed each night. This simple practice has changed my life. Because no matter what happens each day, I go to sleep thinking of something cheerful. . . .

But I am also aware that I am walking without pain. For the first time, I am grateful for each breath in and out—grateful for the gift of life itself. I used to celebrate my birthday every five years and friends' birthdays sometimes. Now I celebrate always. I used to go to sleep worrying about all the things I messed up that day—and trust me that list was often quite long. Now I try really hard to focus on each day's moments of joy.

It is the greatest irony of my life that losing my husband helped me find deeper gratitude—gratitude for the kindness of my friends, the love of my family, the laughter of my children. My hope for you is that you can find that gratitude—not just on the good days, like today, but on the hard ones, when you will really need it.[4]

Recording moments of joy each day was a discipline and a record far beyond my daily practice as a new widow of saying, "Thank you, God, for. . . ." I wish I had a written journal of all those short noontime prayers of gratitude. In 2009 I was grateful simply for the energy to get out of bed in the morning.

The progression from acceptance to gratitude to hope is strong. Without gratitude for the past and the present, we will have difficulty finding hope for the future.

✲

Lesson learned: If we are generous in sharing our time and treasure, gracious in accepting the generosity of others, and thankful for every good gift and kind act, we will—through the grace of God—find the joy of abundant living. Life can be good again.

28

Generosity

I am fully satisfied, now that I have received from Epaphrodi-
tus the gifts you sent, a fragrant offering, a sacrifice acceptable
and pleasing to God. And my God will fully satisfy every need
of yours according to his riches in glory in Christ Jesus. To our
God and Father be glory forever and ever. Amen. Greet every
saint in Christ Jesus. The friends who are with me greet you.
All the saints greet you, especially those of the emperor's house-
hold. The grace of the Lord Jesus Christ be with your spirit.
Philippians 4:18b–23

Grace is a gift, and by definition gifts are freely given, not earned. If they are a payback or reward, a bribe, an exchange, or a contractual act—a *quid pro quo*—they are not gifts. And the grace of God is the greatest gift of all.

The Apostle Paul closed his letter to the Philippians by acknowledging their gift to him. Writing from prison, impoverished, he could not reciprocate. He had no *quid pro quo* to offer. Instead, he acknowledged that theirs was a three-way partnership with God Himself, and he assured the Philippians that God would reward them for their generosity to him.

I had seven decades of practice saying "thank you." From the time I could hold a pencil in my hand, Mama insisted that I write thank-you notes to my grandmothers and aunts for my Christmas and birthday presents. Through that discipline, Mama taught me not to take gifts for granted but to express gratitude for them. As a new widow, I realized that I needed to live my life in gratitude mode, to say "thank you" every day—not only to thank God but also to thank all those who helped me on this journey. In a way, this book is my thank-you note to them. But living life in gratitude mode is about more than saying "thank you." It is also about paying it forward, letting my gratitude overflow on others, being as generous with my time, talent, and treasure as others were toward me.

Everyone in my family would agree that Lev and his mother, Helen, were the most generous people we ever knew. They lavished gifts on those they loved, and Lev in particular loved almost everyone who crossed his path. His memorial service turned into a testimony to his quiet, often secretive gifts—acts of generosity that even I did not always know about.

Lev called himself a "gut giver." When he learned of a need, his first thought was usually, *I can do that.* He reached for his wallet or his checkbook. Early in our marriage, I accused Lev of tipping God, putting a twenty-dollar bill in the offering plate when it was passed, while my parents—living on a railroad pension—habitually gave 10 percent of their income to the church.

Though a church member since childhood, Lev had not grown up in the church. On top of the family's repeated moves, his childhood of boarding school and summer camp kept him from developing ties to a local church. When we married, Lev wanted us to find a church home. As I grew more active in church life, so did he. I watched him slowly fall in love with God, the church, and the people of the church. He no longer tipped God. He gave far beyond the tithe.

Providing for his family was Lev's lifework. Because he had benefited financially from the heartbreakingly early deaths of his father and grandfather, Lev never saw himself as the owner of what he had but merely as the caretaker for future generations. His gratitude for all that he had led to his boundless generosity. Lev IV and Peggy selected the words on his headstone: *Well done, good and faithful steward.* I was keenly aware that all that I had was due to his stewardship and generosity, traits that he first learned from his mother.

Before Christmas each year, Helen drove down from San Antonio with a trunk packed as full of gifts as Santa's sleigh. Then on Christmas Eve, she and Lev's stepfather returned with another carload of gifts. If Lev IV and Peggy gave her a Christmas wish list, she sought to give them everything on the list. When Lev collected antique German beer steins, she bought an entire collection for him.

I often asked for small luxuries that I could not afford to buy for myself. Purses were often on the top of my list, for Helen had superb taste. One unforgettable Christmas I asked for a small brown leather clutch to carry to dinner in the evening—dressy but not an evening bag. On Christmas morning she handed me two beautifully wrapped boxes and told me to take my pick. One was a classic quilted Chanel, the other a Judith Leiber snakeskin with semi-precious stones set in the frame. Many years later, long after my hair turned gray and I quit wearing brown, I shared the story of the Leiber clutch when I passed it on to Cheri, a redhead who often wore brown.

Helen died on March 21, 1996. About seven weeks later, on Mother's Day, as I sat at the kitchen counter eating breakfast, huge tears unexpectedly began to roll down my cheeks, splashing into my cereal bowl. I was overcome by the sad thought, *I'll never have another beautiful purse unless I buy it for myself.* I was not crying over the loss of the gifts. I was crying over the loss of the giver. Afterwards, the pile of gifts under the Christmas tree shrank dramatically. Lev and I became the givers of most of the packages under the tree, and far fewer gifts bore tags with our names on them.

Widowhood thirteen years later brought the reality that I was no longer the most important person in anyone else's life. The pile of gifts under the tree for me dwindled to a tiny handful. Lev IV's and Peggy's top priorities were—as they should be—their spouses and children. Intellectually, I knew that was the way that God intended it to be. Emotionally, I found it hard to accept.

When Helen bought herself something extravagant, she always called it "Helen's gift to Helen." As a widow, I followed her example, giving myself permission to purchase small luxuries from time to time. Then one Friday night at dinner, my friend Maureen wore a spectacular new pearl necklace. When we admired it, she told us it that it was Bill's anniversary gift to her. She explained that each year on her birthday, anniversary, and Christmas, she bought herself the kind of gift that Bill had given her.

I enjoyed "Lev's gifts to Ella" more than my extravagant purchases for myself. They acted as a budgetary control, limiting my major splurges to three, while at the same time allowing me to splurge occasionally. More importantly, they reminded me of the giver, of the source of the gifts.

Most of us find joy in giving to those we love, whether it is a gift of time or of treasure. Reaching beyond our family and friends to give to our neighborhood, our church, our community, and to those in need around the world is a different story. While Helen excelled in giving to those she loved, Lev found ways to make a difference in a much larger arena. While I nudged him to give more, Ralph was his mentor and role model.

When Ralph sold his previous company, he and Jean gave 10 percent of his profit to build a recreation center at our church. When Baylor football was a laughingstock, with little financial support from alumni, they made major commitments of time and money. They gave to every high school graduate and bride in the church. For decades they gave countless hours in ministry to the sick, homebound, and widowed. They lent a helping hand and financial support to scores of people starting a business or experiencing some kind of financial crisis—much of which was never repaid. People mistakenly thought they were enormously wealthy because they gave so much away. No, they were enormously generous.

Sociologists and psychologists have focused on generosity in recent years, measuring its relationship to happiness. Study after study has confirmed that generous people are significantly happier than those who give little or nothing.

The Paradox of Generosity, by Christian Smith and Hillary Davidson, kicked off a spate of research and articles on the subject. Smith and Davidson measured personal well-being by five attributes: happiness, bodily health, purpose in living, avoidance of depression, and interest in personal growth. They ran multiple tests to check their own work. "The key question was: *Is greater generosity, measured in various ways, positively associated with greater well-being?* The clear and consistent answer is 'yes.' Generous practices of different sorts are positively related to greater well-being of different kinds. That positive relationship is not absolute nor overwhelming. But it is clear, consistent, and statistically significant—strong enough to make a real difference in people's lives."[1]

Looking for explanations, they found no correlation between a person's wealth and generosity. Misers, hoarders, and takers exist at every pay grade. While many Americans are exceptionally generous, more give away little, if any, of their time and money; and they are measurably unhappier than the givers in our society.

Generosity cannot be measured only by the amount of money one gives away. I still use the gifts Lev's aunt made us. An excellent seamstress of modest means, she made Lev's Christmas stocking when he was born. When we married, her gift to me was a matching stocking. I still hang those stockings on the mantel every Christmas. My friend Betty gave me a handmade beaded Christmas tree ornament each year. In 1970, when her house was destroyed by a hurricane and she and her husband lived in a trailer with three children and a dog, she still found the time to make an ornament for me. Those gifts that represented so much time proved to be more meaningful and long lasting than luxury items hurriedly purchased at a local store or ordered online.

Gratitude and generosity are two sides of the same coin. A grateful heart leads to a giving spirit. It is the love that the gifts represent, rather than the gifts themselves, that matters so much. Often the intangible gifts of time and talent matter most of all. When we give time to others, we strengthen our relationships; and when we give time to causes and institutions we love, we build new relationships with others who share our values. We find meaning and purpose in living. Ultimately, that is where we find joy.

❁

Lesson learned: A giving spirit flows from the acknowledgment that everything one has is a gift. The open hand of friendship and generosity—not the closed fist that clings tightly to every penny, as well as to every feeling of hurt, anger, bitterness, and unfairness—is the key to joy.

Thank you, God . . .

For surrounding me with your grace;
for granting me the years with Lev;
for hearing my prayers for discernment;
for equipping me with courage to face the future;
for leading me to contentment and purpose;
for lifting my eyes from myself to reclaim joy;
for protecting and unifying my family.
> *for love that overcomes fear,*
> *thank you, God.*

For teaching me to encourage and nurture my children;
for blessing me with examples of unselfishness;
for humbling me that I might learn and grow;
for answering my prayers for serenity;
for guiding me to a place that led from grief to joy;
for providing me with loving, caring friends;
for presenting opportunities to give and receive hospitality.
> *for unity that strengthens relationships,*
> *thank you, God.*

For supplying moments of joy in the midst of deepest grief;
for warning me of those who were false friends;
for showing me what really matters in life;
for giving me a mother-in-law who lived life to the fullest;
for empowering me with confidence to meet responsibilities;

for furnishing role models who demonstrated how to live;
for promising eternal life that I might anticipate reunion
  with loved ones.

> *for maturity that brings wisdom,*
> *thank you, God.*

For strengthening my family and drawing us together;
for cautioning me to balance strength with gentleness;
for moving me from fear and anxiety to peace;
for filling me with a good and worthy attitude;
for enabling me to accept my circumstances;
for overwhelming me with abundant life;
for opening my hands and heart in generosity.

> *for the peace that leads to joy,*
> *thank you, God.*

> *Amen.*

Select Bibliography

Accettura, Mark. "18 Recommendations for Minimizing Inheritance Conflict." *AAII Journal.* April 2012. http://www. aaii.com/journal/article/19-recommendations-for-minimizing-inheritance-conflict.mobile.

Alexander, Elizabeth. *The Light of the World: A Memoir.* New York: Grand Central, 2015. eBook.

Black, Elizabeth Head. *Hand in Hand: Walking with the Psalms through Loneliness.* Houston: Bright Sky Press, 2014.

Bonanno, George A. *The Other Side of Sadness: What the New Science of Bereavement Tells Us about Life after Loss.* New York: Basic Books, 2009. eBook.

Brody, Elaine M. "On Being Very, Very Old: An Insider's Perspective." *The Gerontologist* 50, no. 1 (2010): 2–10.

———. *Women in the Middle: Their Parent Care Years.* 2nd ed. Springer Series on Lifestyles and Issues in Aging. New York: Springer, 2004.

Brooks, David. *The Road to Character.* New York: Random House, 2015.

Claypool, John R. *Tracks of a Fellow Struggler: Living and Growing through Grief.* Rev. ed. Harrisburg, Pa.: Morehouse Publishing, 2004 [1995]. eBook.

Cuddy, Amy. *Presence: Bringing Your Boldest Self to Your Biggest Challenges.* New York: Little, Brown, 2015. eBook.

De Tocqueville, Alexis. *Democracy in America.* Translated by Henry Reeves. East Sussex, U.K.: Vigo Books, 2012 [1840]. eBook.

Didion, Joan. *The Year of Magical Thinking.* New York: Alfred A. Knopf, 2006. eBook.

Downes, John, and Jordan Elliot Goodman. *Finance and Investment Handbook.* 9th ed. Hauppauge, N.Y.: Barron's Educational Series, Inc., 2014 [1986].

Druckerman, Pamela. "Learning How to Exert Self-Control." *New York Times,* 14 Sept 2014.

Duckworth, Angela. *Grit: The Power of Passion and Perseverance.* New York: Scribner, 2016. eBook.

Dweck, Carol S. *Mindset: The New Psychology of Success.* New York: Random House, 2006. eBook.

Eswaran, Mukesh. *Why Gender Matters in Economics.* Princeton, N.J.: Princeton University Press, 2014. eBook.

Fleet, Carole Brody, with Syd Harriet. *Widows Wear Stilettos: A Practical and Emotional Guide for the Young Widow.* Far Hills, N.J.: New Horizon Press, 2009. eBook.

Garland, David E. "Philippians." In *Ephesians–Philemon.* The Expositor's Bible Commentary 12, edited by Tremper Longman III and David E. Garland. Grand Rapids: Zondervan, 2006.

Ginsburg, Genevieve Davis. *Widow to Widow: Thoughtful, Practical Ideas for Rebuilding Your Life.* Rev. ed. Cambridge, Mass.: Da Capo Press, 1995. eBook.

Graham, Katherine. *Personal History.* New York: Alfred A. Knopf, 1997.

Guiliano, Mireille. *Women, Work and the Art of Savoir Faire: Business Sense and Sensibility.* New York: Atria Books, 2009. eBook.

Harris, Melissa, and Julie Wernau. "Fortune's Fate." *Chicago Tribune,* 18 Dec 2011.

Hirsch, Edward. *Gabriel: A Poem.* New York: Alfred A. Knopf, 2014.

———. "A Poet On Losing His Son: 'Before You Heal, You Have To Mourn.'" By David Greene. Poetry. NPR.org. 5 Sept 2014. http://www.npr.org/2014/09/05/345796530/a-poet-on-losing-his-son-before-you-heal-you-have-to-mourn.

Kaufman, Sarah L. *The Art of Grace: On Moving Well through Life.* New York: W. W. Norton, 2016. eBook.

Keith-Lucas, Alan. *Giving and Taking Help.* Chapel Hill: University of North Carolina Press, 1972.

Khullar, Dhruv. "Loneliness Is a Health Hazard, but There Are Remedies." *New York Times*, 22 Dec 2016. https://www.nytimes.com/2016/12/22/upshot/how-social-isolation-is-killing-us.html.

Kleberg, Sally S. *The Stewardship of Private Wealth: Managing Personal and Family Financial Assets.* New York: McGraw-Hill, 1997.

Lewis, C. S. *A Grief Observed.* New York: HarperCollins, 1961. eBook.

———. *Mere Christianity.* New York: HarperCollins, 1952. eBook.

———. *The Problem of Pain.* New York: HarperCollins, 1940. eBook.

———. *Surprised by Joy: The Shape of My Early Life.* Boston: Houghton Mifflin Harcourt, 1955. eBook.

Lindbergh, Anne Morrow. *Gift from the Sea.* New York: Pantheon Books, 1955. eBook.

McRaven, William H. *Make Your Bed: Little Things That Can Change Your Life . . . and Maybe the World.* New York: Grand Central Publishing, 2017. eBook.

Mischel, Walter. *The Marshmallow Test: Mastering Self-Control.* New York: Little, Brown, 2014. eBook.

Morris, Jonathan. *The Way of Serenity: Finding Peace and Happiness in the Serenity Prayer.* San Francisco: HarperOne, 2014. eBook.

Newport, Frank. *God Is Alive and Well: The Future of Religion in America.* New York: Gallup Press, 2012.

Noonan, Peggy. "Cantor Bows Out With Grace." *Wall Street Journal*, 12 June 2014.

Oates, Joyce Carol. *A Widow's Story: A Memoir*. New York: HarperCollins, 2011. eBook.

Phillips, J. B., trans. *The New Testament in Modern English*. Rev. ed. New York: Galahad Books, 1995.

Piper, Watty. *The Little Engine That Could*. New York: Platt and Munk, 1930.

Rehm, Diane. *On My Own*. New York: Alfred A. Knopf, 2016. eBook.

Roberts, Abishai W. *Abishai W. Roberts Papers*, Mss. 370. Louisiana and Lower Mississippi Valley Collections, Special Collections. Hill Memorial Library, Louisiana State University Libraries, Baton Rouge.

Sacks, Oliver. *Gratitude*. New York: Alfred A. Knopf, 2015. eBook.

Sandberg, Sheryl, and Adam Grant. *Option B: Facing Adversity, Building Resilience, and Finding Joy*. New York: Alfred A. Knopf, 2017. eBook.

Smith, Christian, and Hilary Davidson. *The Paradox of Generosity: Giving We Receive, Grasping We Lose*. Oxford, U.K.: Oxford University Press, 2014. eBook.

Starr, Ken. "Ken Starr, Board of Contributors: Rejoicing in the Spirit, Human and Divine, All Around Us at Christmas and Beyond." *Waco Tribune-Herald*, 24 Dec 2014.

Tergesen, Ann. "Why Everything You Think about Aging May Be Wrong: As We Get Older, Friendships, Creativity and Satisfaction with Life Can Flourish." *Wall Street Journal*, 30 Nov 2014.

Tuhy, Carrie. "Just Saying 'Yes': Joyce Carol Oates." *Publishers Weekly*, 18 Feb 2013.

Williams, Roy, and Vic Preisser. *Preparing Heirs: Five Steps to a Successful Transition of Family Wealth and Values*. San Francisco: Robert D. Reed, 2003.

About the Author

For forty-six years Ella enjoyed her life as a wife, mother, and volunteer. All that changed when her husband died in 2009 after a lengthy illness. Ella became the completely unqualified president of Prichard Oil Company. While learning the business and settling the estate in the midst of the Great Recession, she poured out her grief and anxiety on Twitter and Facebook. Readers responded, "Keep writing." The idea for *Reclaiming Joy*—inspired by the Apostle Paul's letter to the Philippians—began to germinate during a trip to Nantucket in August 2013. A year later, Ella started writing about her journey from grief to joy—a project that consumed her time and energy for more than three years.

Born in New Orleans in 1941, Ella grew up in Texarkana, Arkansas. Shy and studious, she fell in love with words on paper as a young child. Books were her best friends, and the nearby public library was her favorite destination. Without any formal training in journalism, she regularly produced little mimeographed newspapers for the groups she belonged to. She served as editor of her high school newspaper. With the encouragement of her English/journalism teacher and the local newspaper editor, she enrolled at Baylor University, Waco, Texas, in 1959 with plans to pursue a newspaper career. Those plans were abandoned when she met Lev while working as a summer intern reporter at the *Corpus Christi Caller-Times* in 1962. They married five months later.

After her graduation from Baylor in 1963, Ella found myriad ways to share her talent through church and community service: writing Sunday School curriculum for the Southern Baptist Convention Sunday School Board (now LifeWay), writing and editing for local nonprofits, and producing promotional materials for nonprofit capital campaigns. Known as a gourmet cook, she served as coeditor of *Fiesta: Favorite Recipes of South Texas*, a top-selling cookbook published by the Junior League of Corpus Christi. At the same time, she stayed actively involved in the lives of her two children, Lev IV and Peggy, and later with their spouses and her four grandchildren.

Ella blogs at www.ellawallprichard.com, where other resources on widowhood can be found. You may contact her at her website to book speaking and teaching engagements.

Notes

The Valley of the Shadow of Death
1   John 14:18, 26, 27.

1 ~ Grace
1   Helen Harris, assistant professor, Diana R. Garland School of Social Work, Baylor University, interview by the author, Waco, Texas, 8 May 2015, and subsequent emails.

2   Edward Hirsch, "A Poet On Losing His Son: 'Before You Heal, You Have To Mourn,'" interview by David Greene, *Poetry*, NPR. org, 5 Sep 2014, http://www.npr.org/2014/09/05/345796530/a-poet-on-losing-his-son-before-you-heal-you-have-to-mourn.

3   Joyce Carol Oates, *A Widow's Story: A Memoir* (New York: HarperCollins, 2011), eBook.

2 ~ Gratitude
1   Watty Piper, *The Little Engine That Could* (New York: Platt and Munk, 1930).

2   Carrie Tuhy, "Just Saying 'Yes': Joyce Carol Oates," *Publishers Weekly*, 18 Feb 2013.

3   Genevieve Davis Ginsburg, *Widow to Widow: Thoughtful, Practical Ideas for Rebuilding Your Life*, rev. ed. (Cambridge, Mass.: Da Capo Press, 1997), eBook.

4   Don Moen, "Give Thanks" (New York: Sony/ATV Music Publishing LLC, 1986), song.

3 ~ Insight
1   David E. Garland, "Philippians," in *Ephesians–Philemon*, ed. Tremper Longman III and David E. Garland, The Expositor's Bible Commentary 12 (Grand Rapids: Zondervan, 2006), 195,

196. Garland's commentary has informed nearly all my writing related to Philippians, and I gratefully acknowledge this book's reliance on his scholarship and insight.

4 ~ Courage

1 The Frenchman Alexis De Toqueville was the first to identify American enlightened self-interest in his 1840 book *Democracy in America*, translated by Henry Reeves (East Sussex, U.K.: Vigo Books, 2012), chap. 8, eBook.

2 David Brooks, *The Road to Character* (New York: Random House, 2015), 29, 30.

3 Brooks, *Road to Character*, 269, 270.

5 ~ Expectations

1 The best man at our wedding offered the traditional Mexican wedding toast at our rehearsal dinner: "*Salud, dinero, y amor... y tiempo para disfrutarios!* Health, wealth, and love . . . and time to enjoy them." He offered it again at Lev IV and Cheri's rehearsal dinner, and I toasted my grandson and his bride with the same words in 2012.

2 Joan Didion, *The Year of Magical Thinking* (New York: Alfred A. Knopf, 2006), eBook.

3 Walter Mischel is quoted by Pamela Druckerman in an interview, "Learning How to Exert Self-Control," *New York Times*, 14 Sep 2014.

4 Carol S. Dweck, *Mindset: The New Psychology of Success* (New York: Random House, 2006), chap. 2, eBook.

5 Elaine M. Brody, "On Being Very, Very Old: An Insider's Perspective," *The Gerontologist* 50, no. 1 (2010): 2–10.

6 ~ Joy

1 Frank Newport, *God Is Alive and Well: The Future of Religion in America* (New York: Gallup Press, 2012), 125–27.

2 "ACS Demographic and Housing Estimates: 2009–2013 American Community Survey 5-Year Estimates," American Fact Finder, United States Census Bureau, accessed 8 Jun 2015, http://factfinder.census.gov/faces/tableservices/jsf/pages/productview.xhtml?pid=ACS_13_5YR_DP05&src=pt.

3 Elaine M. Brody, *Women in the Middle: Their Parent Care Years*, 2nd ed., Springer Series on Lifestyles and Issues in Aging (New York: Springer, 2004), 34, 35.

4 Alan Keith-Lucas, *Giving and Taking Help* (Chapel Hill: University of North Carolina Press, 1972), cited by Helen Harris.

5   Harris, interview.

7 ~ Unity

1   Clemons' study is discussed in Roy Williams and Vic Preisser, *Preparing Heirs: Five Steps to a Successful Transition of Family Wealth and Values* (San Francisco: Robert D. Reed, 2003).

8 ~ Encouragement

1   Philippians 2:1-4, J. B. Phillips, trans., *The New Testament in Modern English*, rev. ed. (New York: Galahad Books, 1995), 412.

2   Mark Accettura, "18 Recommendations for Minimizing Inheritance Conflict," *AAII Journal* (Apr 2012), http://www.aaii.com/journal/article/19-recommendations-for-minimizing-inheritance-conflict.mobile.

9 ~ Unselfishness

1   Abishai W. Roberts Papers, mss. 370, Louisiana and Lower Mississippi Valley Collections, Special Collections, Hill Memorial Library, Louisiana State University Libraries, Baton Rouge.

2   Sally S. Kleberg, *The Stewardship of Private Wealth: Managing Personal and Family Financial Assets* (New York: McGraw-Hill, 1997), 20, 21.

3   Helen Howarth Lemmon, "Turn Your Eyes Upon Jesus," 1922, song.

10 ~ Humility

1   Humility is an underlying theme in Brooks' book *Road to Character* and is described in detail in the "Introduction: Adam II." It has informed my writing in this chapter.

2   Jonathan Morris, *The Way of Serenity: Finding Peace and Happiness in the Serenity Prayer* (San Francisco: HarperOne, 2014), eBook.

11 ~ Serenity

1   The Serenity Prayer was inspired by a longer, more profound, untitled prayer written by American theologian Reinhold Niebuhr sometime before 1943.

13 ~ Friendship

1   Dhruv Khullar, "Loneliness Is a Health Hazard, but There Are Remedies," *New York Times*, 22 Dec 2016, https://www.nytimes.com/2016/12/22/upshot/how-social-isolation-is-killing-us.html.

2   John Pavlovitz, "The Grieving You Need Most after the Funeral," *John Pavlovitz: Stuff That Needs to Be Said* (blog), 5 Jan 2017, https://johnpavlovitz.com/2017/01/05/the-grieving-need-you-most-after-the-funeral/.

14 ~ Hospitality

1   *Fiesta: Favorite Recipes of South Texas* (Corpus Christi, Texas: The Junior League of Corpus Christi, 1973).
2   C. S. Lewis, *Surprised by Joy: The Shape of My Early Life* (Boston: Houghton Mifflin Harcourt, 1955), eBook.
3   Randall Stone and Dan Clay, "6 Tips for Designing Happiness," *Co.Design*, 10 June 2015, https://www.fastcodesign.com/3047190/6-tips-for-designing-happiness.

16 ~ Beware!

1   Oates, *Widow's Story*, 540–42 (emphasis original).
2   Turock's philosophy is discussed in Ken Blanchard and Steve Gottry, *The On-Time, On-Target Manager: How a "Last-Minute Manager" Conquered Procrastination* (New York: HarperCollins, 2004), 82.

17 ~ Priorities

1   Eric Cantor is quoted by Peggy Noonan in "Cantor Bows Out With Grace," *Wall Street Journal*, 12 June 2014, print.

18 ~ Maturity

1   A slightly revised text of Ken Starr's speech was printed in the *Waco Tribune-Herald*, "Rejoicing in the Spirit, Human and Divine, All Around Us at Christmas and Beyond," 24 Dec 2014, print.
2   Khullar, "Loneliness." See chap. 13, "Friendship," for a more detailed summary of the article.

19 ~ Confidence

1   Katherine Graham, *Personal History* (New York: Alfred A. Knopf, 1997), chaps. 18, 28.

20 ~ Role Models

1   Diane Rehm, *On My Own* (New York: Knopf, 2016), eBook.
2   Harris, interview.

21 ~ Anticipation

1   George A. Bonanno, *The Other Side of Sadness: What the New Science of Bereavement Tells Us about Life after Loss* (New York: Basic Books, 2009), chap. 10, eBook.

2 Didion, *Magical Thinking*, 126.

3 Rehm, *On My Own*, 85, 86.

22 ~ Strength

1 John R. Claypool, *Tracks of a Fellow Struggler: Living and Growing through Grief*, rev. ed. (Harrisburg, Pa.: Morehouse Publishing, 2004 [1995]), eBook.

2 Claypool, *Tracks*, 53.

3 Melissa Harris and Julie Wernau, "Fortune's Fate," *Chicago Tribune*, 18 Dec 2011, print.

23 ~ Gentleness

1 Sarah L. Kaufman, *The Art of Grace: On Moving Well through Life* (New York: W. W. Norton, 2016), eBook.

2 Garland, "Philippians," 252, 253.

24 ~ Peace

1 Garland, "Philippians," 253.

2 Lidie H. Edmonds, "My Faith Has Found a Resting Place," 1891, song.

25 ~ Attitude

1 Amy Cuddy, *Presence: Bringing Your Boldest Self to Your Biggest Challenges* (New York: Little, Brown, 2015), eBook. Cuddy's research parallels my discoveries about the effectiveness of "fake it until you become it."

2 Ann Tergesen cites the research of Caura Carstensen, director of the Stanford University Center of Longevity, "Why Everything You Think about Aging May Be Wrong: As We Get Older, Friendships, Creativity and Satisfaction with Life Can Flourish," *Wall Street Journal*, 30 Nov 2014, print.

27 ~ Abundance

1 Garland, "Philippians," 257.

2 Michael Hyatt, "Why Giving Thanks Gives You an Edge," *Your Virtual Mentor* (blog), accessed 13 Apr 2017, https://michaelhyatt.com/why-giving-thanks-gives-you-an-edge.html.

3 Judy Brizendine, "Three-Legged Stool Is Crucial, Particularly during Tough Times (like Grief)," *Stunned by Grief* (blog), accessed 13 Apr 2017, http://stunnedbygrief.com/stunned-by-grief/three-legged-stool-crucial-particularly-tough-times-like-grief/.

4 Sheryl Sandberg, transcript of her commencement address at the University of California, Berkeley, 14 May 2016, Time.com,

http://time.com/money/4337611/transcript-sheryl-sandberg-commencement-berkeley/.

28 ~ Generosity

1   Christian Smith and Hilary Davidson, *The Paradox of Generosity: Giving We Receive, Grasping We Lose* (Oxford, U.K.: Oxford University Press, 2014), chap. 1, eBook.

Index

144; accepting, 5, 11, 46, 60; division of, 55. *See also* family business; fiduciary
retirement, 85
role models, 11, 22, 27, 32, 69, 90, 98, 127, 139–45, 189. *See also* mentors

saints of the church, 77
Sandberg, Sheryl, 195
Scripture, xii. *See also* John, Gospel of; Philippians, Paul's letter to the; Psalms
security, 120
self-centeredness, 60
self-discipline, 144
self-interest, 24, 57, 163, 192
serenity, 73–79
Serenity Prayer, 74
settled happiness, 27, 175. *See also* joy
sharks, 114
Simon, Sidney B., 193
sinkholes, 8, 38, 40, 70, 79, 84, 103, 131, 147
sisterhood, 93, 130, 144, 192. *See also* friendship; relationships
smiling spouse, 36, 115, 156
social media: blogs, 130, 182, 195; Facebook, 166, 182–83
Social Security, 61, 94
socializing, 12, 90, 94, 130, 180, 194. *See also* entertaining; hospitality; hostess, hosting
solitude, 69–70, 79, 84, 87, 170. *See also* loneliness

sound mind and body, 10, 59
spiritual desert, xvii, 172
Starr, Ken, 128
stay-at-home moms, 9
stay-at-home wives, 60, 94
stewardship, 125, 199
Stone, Randall, 102
strength, 155–60
stress, 108, 156

taxes, xi; income, xii, 135; property, 117
Texarkana, Arkansas, 23, 63, 89, 129
thoughtfulness, 193
traditions, 111, 157, 192
travel, 82–84, 85–87, 171
trustees, 4, 36, 43, 46, 135. *See also* advisors, financial; bankers
trusts, 44–46
Turock, Art, 118
unity, 43–49
unselfishness, 59–65

U.S. Census, 36

Waco, Texas, 23, 90, 129, 173
Wall Street Journal, 5
Williamsburg, Virginia, 25, 83, 86, 90, 181. *See also* Colonial Williamsburg Foundation
willpower, 22
wisdom, 126